The bonfire of well-being

Unleash your Inner Fire, Fan the Flames, and Embrace a Life of Vibrant Well-Being

Dr. Jaime Leal

Emotional Paycheck Publishing

On that fateful day, August 8, 2021, as you lay in the hospital, you sent me a message of love and pride. In those precious words, you expressed your unwavering support and affection, proclaiming yourself **the happiest man on earth**. Little did I know that those would be the last words I would hear from you.

Today, I stand before my readers not only as an expert in happiness in the workplace but also as the son of the happiest man on earth. This book is a testament to the legacy you left behind and a tribute to the incredible influence you had on my life.

This one is for you, Dad. Your love, strength, and happiness will forever be my guiding light.

Jaimito

Credits

Author: Jaime Leal
Website: www.emotionalpaycheck.com
Graphic Design and Cover Art: Jaime Leal
Illustrations: Damgilex, Diana Nezhivova, and Jaime Leal
Author's Photograph: Daniela Lisi

ISBN: 978-1-7778473-3-3

First edition, 2023

Disclaimer & Copyright

The views and opinions expressed in this book are those of the author and do not necessarily reflect the views of the publisher or any other entity. The information contained in this book is provided for informational purposes only and is not intended as legal, financial, or professional advice. The author and publisher are not responsible for any errors or omissions in the book, and the reader should seek appropriate professional advice before taking any actions based on the information contained in this book. This book is not intended to diagnose, treat, or cure medical or mental health conditions. Please consult a qualified healthcare professional before changing your treatment or care.

Names and trademarks

In this book, we will use the names Canadian Institute of Emotional Paycheck, Emotional Paycheck Institute of Canada, Canadian Institute of Salario Emocional (Emotional Salary), and Emotional Paycheck interchangeably to refer to the specialized institute in well-being and emotional salary and its methodology. The terms Emotional Paycheck®, Salario Emocional® (Emotional Salary), and Tarrix® are intellectual property and properly registered trademarks of their owner, Jaime Leal.

The official name of the institute is Emotional Paycheck Institute of Canada, located in Ontario, Canada.

Emotional Paycheck®
Institute Of Canada

Contents

Introduction 1

1. Happiness 5
2. Definitions of happiness 13
3. The Fantastic 4 of happiness 35
4. The bonfire of wellbeing 47
5. Your bonfire elements 57
   - Social SPW
   - Community SPW
   - Career SPW
   - Physical-Emotional SPW
   - Financial SPW
   - Spiritual SPW
6. Putting it all together 87
7. The triangles of wellbeing 91
   - Social welfare triangle
   - Triangle of well-being at work
   - Personal wellness triangle
8. Lighting the bonfire 115
9. Leadership of well-being 123

Conclusion 131
About the Author 135
References 137
Chapter 151

Introduction

WHY IS THIS BOOK IMPORTANT?

In the past few years, businesses and governments from different countries have started increasing their efforts to improve the well-being of their employees and citizens, respectively. Not long ago, people were considered just another asset of an organization and, therefore, were treated just as a number (some companies still do this). However, employees are now regarded as individuals in many multinational corporations and companies from various industries. We have taken great strides in well-being at work, yet, there still is a long way to go.

The times when some leaders had a group of thugs who violently subdued those who did not comply with the rules are long gone. Today, workers have rights. They know them and make them respected. We have progressed!

Governments increasingly talk about well-being. Some, such as the Kingdom of Bhutan, have been radical by ceasing to measure Gross Domestic Product (GDP) and instead measuring Gross National Happiness (GNH). As a result, we often see lists of countries competing for the highest rank in the happiness index.

However, **neither a government nor an entire country can make a person happy.** They can only aspire to prepare the basics for individual well-being but cannot make a person happy. Happiness is a personal task, which is why this book is necessary.

The Bonfire of Wellbeing is intended to allow you to understand the essential elements required to ignite the flame of happiness. Of course, these elements are different in each individual. Still, they can be classified into six general categories explained in this book.

Contrary to what we see daily in the news, well-being is present in most environments; people live better and healthier than ever, and access to better medicine and information is available for anyone who wishes to learn. So, what is stopping you from being happy?

You may be missing one of the six essential categories of well-being. So, sit comfortably and read this book as I explain the well-being categories required to ignite the flame of happiness. Discover which ones you need to strengthen and how, and decide once and for all to be happy, and decide once and for all to be happy. After all, no one can do it for you!

The concept of happiness is an ethereal enigma, teasing us like a shimmering mirage in the desert. Just as we believe we are nearing its captivating embrace, happiness transforms, eluding our grasp and revealing itself in new, unforeseen forms.

Dr. Leal

1

Happiness

A Brief Story

Based on this story, you may be able to calculate my age! It was the summer of 1979 (Awoooooooo!). I used to spend my afternoons by the only telephone booth of the López Mateos housing complex, a small town located on the slopes of Cerro de las Mitras in Nuevo León, a settlement isolated from all communication and which could only be accessed through a dirt road of around five kilometres. Only one bus line could take you to the area, and the bus driver was "Don Tito."

The streets were named using numbers and did not exceed twenty. It was, indeed, a small town which complied with the widespread belief: "Small town, big hell." Wow, we heard new, crazy stories daily!

In the seventies, there were no cell phones, and a land-line phone was reserved for the wealthiest classes. But, of course, those families didn't live in or around my neigh-bourhood. We were so poor that I remember having school-mates who attended classes barefoot and others who wore worn-out uniforms. Even though the food was always abundant at home, I was very aware that my parents made a monumental effort to ensure me and my sister always had what we needed.

We quite literally lived on the mountain's slopes, which I now value very much because it helped me explore the world much more freely than those born in the city. I walked in the mountains, played for hours lost in the fields, rode horses I thought had no owner, and got lost on more than one occasion riding a bicycle with my friends. We were free!

In "La López", as we affectionately called our neighbourhood, there was only one phone booth. It was located among the dusty oaks and leafy sycamores of a triangular plaza on Calle 11 in a small kiosk with the only real-time connection with the outside world. The phone!

The telephone bell used to ring so loud it could be heard several feet away. The operator assigned to answer the calls had a voice as powerful as the best stage actors. "Buenoooo!" (Hello). She would scream with substance whenever she answered a call.

My mission was simple: Wait for someone from the neighbourhood to receive a call, listen carefully to the recipient's address, and shoot out on my bicycle to deliver the news in exchange for what was, most times, some monetary gratification. That's right; they didn't always pay me with money; on some occasions, they gave me some candy and other times, they gave me some fruit or said: "Thank you!" (As you can see, I sometimes got paid only in emotional paychecks).

I started saving money and soon bought some accessories for my bike. Then, I bought my mechanical horn, activated by pressing a plastic bulb and making a sound I loved. I also purchased a bigger mirror I had fun with and some little metal tubes that I could attach to the rear tires of my bike to give my friends a ride ("Little devils," we called them). **I was only seven years old, and my happiness was my bicycle!**

The courier business was booming. We were just two or three "freelance" couriers who provided the service until Kike arrived, a neighbour and schoolmate who, taking advantage of being older, more muscular and much less empathetic than me, threatened to hit me if I arrived before him to leave a message. My business was over, and all in a violent way!

At first, I ignored him. I kept delivering messages, but Kike kept his word and beat me several times. He also broke the mirror I had bought for my bike. Good luck with my misfortune! My business was gone.

Kike was not satisfied only with hitting me in the afternoon, but he would also do so during school hours, chasing me every time we met during recess.

My dad noticed I was being bullied and enlisted me in Tae Kwon Do classes. Since I was a shy boy and fearful as heck, I was punched by Kike in the morning at school and kicked in the afternoon during my Tae Kwon Do classes. What a torture!

I was seven years old, and although I still loved my bike, my definition of happiness had dramatically changed; **my true happiness, at the time, was not meeting Kike at school recess and surviving my Tae Kwon Do classes**.

I had two great friends that I still keep, Hugo and Ulises (legendary names, I know), and they were my heroes. They consistently defended me from the beatings of Kike. Still, as expected, they were not always present. Hence, the latter convinced me, and I abandoned my career as the fastest messenger in the neighbourhood.

Time passed, but my desire to work did not die, so I changed my line of business: I became a baker. Well, not exactly, but I started working in a bakery. I was barely nine years old and was allowed to bag bread for customers; in exchange, customers would give me a tip and, at the end of the day, the owner of the bakery, Doña Norma, allowed me to take some bread home as payment for my workday.

I fondly remember the beautiful moments when I would come home, and my mother and I would share a piece of bread with a glass of milk. **Forget the bike: my happiness was to see my mother's proud look!**

As I grew up, I had a few more jobs. I helped care for some animals, distributed newspapers, and even sold the sweets I collected at my friends' parties. Yes, I collected the best candies from my friends' goodie bags and sold them later. There's always been an entrepreneur in me. Eventually, and in between gigs, I graduated from high school.

I was 17 years old and worked selling cleaning supplies that I delivered in a car that my father had gifted me. I saved every penny I earned and dreamed of buying my own car, a Volkswagen Sedan (in Mexico, we call them "bochitos"). It was going to be red, with racing-style seats, a powerful stereo, and speakers that, in my dreams, were already playing the latest hits by ACDC. Like many teenagers, I no longer spent so much time at home, I no longer had dinner with my mother... Now I had more banal tastes, and **my happiness was fixed**

on buying that car!

In addition to my job as a seller of cleaning products, I sold leather clothing, belts, bags and exotic boots, which allowed me to raise enough money in less than a year to buy my bochito.

It wasn't red, but it was light blue. Some pieces with rust, the white interiors with the odd stain that I would try to remove with detergent, and a broken exhaust, something that I planned to solve with a mechanic friend whom we called "Pecas." (Freckles)

I still remember my nerves counting the money before the seller: one... two... three, I counted with trembling hands. Then, finally, I got into the shiny bochito I had bought just a few minutes ago. I drove out, and right before me, another similar car stopped.

It was also a bochito, light blue, with white interiors, almost the same as mine, but this one had sport wheels and wider tires. Guess what I thought? That's right; I thought, "I want those tires!" I had barely managed to buy my car, and there I was; **my happiness had already changed!** Does that sound familiar?

Thus, without realizing it, our definition of happiness is so dynamic that it becomes virtually impossible to accurately describe it, let alone claim to understand someone else's definition of happiness. The search for happiness is a personal task where you can receive advice and ideas, but you must do all the heavy lifting. Understanding what makes you happy at any moment can make a big difference in your life and those around you.

What is happiness? What a question! We should try to concretize this issue and be more specific with what we are asking since what makes you happy at some point in your life may not do so at another. Our definition of happiness changes!

But we must start somewhere, so for now; I invite you to take a break from reading, find a quiet place, reserve at least five minutes without interruptions and prepare your favourite drink to answer the following question:

At this point in your life, what makes you happy?

Answering this question is the first step towards a happier you, so take your time and be as specific as possible.

In most cases, when we inquire about a person's desires in life, their response invariably includes happiness. However, when pressed to articulate the essence of happiness, an eerie silence fills the air. It is as though we ardently yearn for happiness without pausing to contemplate its profound meaning.

Dr. Leal

2

Definitions of happiness

THROUGHOUT HISTORY

Although the vast majority of human beings seek happiness in their lives, we rarely stop to analyze the meaning of that term. As I explore in detail in my book The Emotional Paycheck Method, happiness is a widely used term but often unexplored.

Generally speaking, chances are that if you ask someone what they want in life, that person will list happiness as one of those things they desire. But if you ask them what happiness is, they will become silent! So, it seems that many of us are superficially satisfied just with wishing for happiness, whatever that means, without a clear "why," just because. However, many historical figures have devoted their attention to such a valuable topic.

Next, I'll paraphrase some of the greatest thinkers in human history who took a moment in their research to address the subject of happiness. Let's see which of them you identify with the most.

From *Lao Tzu (601 BC-531 BC)*, we can learn to live in the present, avoiding the depression caused by past events that cannot be changed and the anxiety about a future we do not yet inhabit and probably will never happen. For Lao Tzu, we can infer happiness is found by living in the present. If he is correct, should we stop dwelling on the past? Should we stop planning for the future?

A well-known Japanese story tells of two celibate monks, *Tanzan* and *Ekido*, returning to their monastery after going to town for some provisions. They walked along a winding road between the mountains when torrential rain came. The river, which had grown mighty from the rain, covered the small bridge they would have used to cross to the other side. After a while, they saw a young woman dressed in a gorgeous silk kimono hesitate to cross the bridge, evidently fearful of being carried away by the rising waters.

Without a second thought, *Tanzan* came to her aid, carried her into his arms, and crossed the stream, leaving her safe and sound on the other side of the path. *Ekido* remained silent, visibly upset, for the rest of the way.

Finally, when they reached the monastery door, *Ekido* let out all his angry complaints:

"Monks are not supposed to touch women, especially if they are beautiful and young like the one you carried over the water. I don't know how you could commit such a severe infraction," *Ekido* said repeatedly.

Ekido's complaint and angry words surprised *Tanzan*, who had completely forgotten about the incident. He looked into *Ekido's* eyes and said:

"It's true. I crossed that woman across the river. It was barely a few meters; however, it seems that you're still carrying her." (End of the story)

How many times do we end up experiencing the same painful events from the past over and over again when we bring them back to memory?

Without realizing it, **we fan the flame of resentment by remembering some disdain from a loved one, we keep alive the frustration felt by that one missed opportunity, and we blame ourselves thousands of times for the same mistake we made in the past.** Does it sound familiar to you?

On the following scale, give this great thinker your "review" (yes, like people do in Google®'s reviews). How much do you agree with Lao-Tzu?

How difficult is it for you to forget the past? Are you one of those who think that failing to remember the past exposes us to repeating it? If so, would it help you to feel a little more like Lao Tzu? Before answering, come with me to learn from the Buddha himself.

It is attributed to *Siddhartha Gautama (Buddha)*, who lived around 500 BC, that there is no path to happiness because happiness is the path itself. Hence, we can infer that happiness is life with all its nuances for Buddha. If so, should anything make us happy?

The year was 2010, and my business as a corporate trainer was blooming. I had my own home, fully paid, a business in the wealthiest municipality in the country, nice cars, trucks and even three motorcycles at once; I could as well be flying my paraglider or enjoying a break in a country plot of several hectares I had bought in the same town where my father was born. I even considered buying a small plane to travel with my family; money was not an issue!

As a psychologist, I travelled doing what I liked, participated in various humanitarian aid organizations and spent my weekends deciding which of my hobbies would occupy my days off. What a life!

As a volunteer, I went to a humanitarian rescue mission in Haiti, helped hundreds of people after the tragedy, and received the Exemplary Citizen award in my city. What more could I ask for? I was the pride of my family. **What a fortune mine was!**

The month of October arrived. I had been working late in my office and stopped for water on the way home. I felt someone push me from behind as I left the convenience store. I fell to the floor and, when I tried to stand up, I felt a plastic bag on my face. The rest is history. **I was kidnapped.**

I feared for my family and spent nights weeping as I lay half-naked in a stinking room. I was anxious about knowing what would happen to my life, my family, what would become of my parents, and how my children would remember me. **I was about to die!**

Amid that uncertainty, the only sure thing was that my bank account was getting emptier and emptier. I was losing my money, and potentially I would lose my life. **"What a fortune mine is!"** I told myself several times during the more than seven days I spent in captivity.

I negotiated my release, and as soon as they let me go, I emigrated to Canada. However, I kept the kidnapping and the financial ruin I was facing a secret, fearing retaliation and struggling with paranoia due to my PTSD (post-traumatic stress disorder).

I moved to Ontario, where I started from scratch. I took my first steps in what I called "The Hero's Path," that of the migrant who sacrifices for a better future for the next generations.

I spent sleepless days and nights struggling to build a new business in an unfamiliar land with no contacts and limited resources. I was still battered by post-traumatic stress from my abduction. In Monterrey, I was recognized on the streets. I wrote for the most popular newspaper and even appeared on a state television channel. Yet, in Canada, I was a nobody. **What a fortune mine was!**

I began exploring new markets due to my fear of returning to Mexico. That was how Ecuador opened the door for me. After that, my hard work took me to Colombia and later to Guatemala. I continued with Puerto Rico, Nicaragua, Spain, the Netherlands and eighteen other countries. **That's how I became international.**

Ironically, my fear of returning to Mexico pushed me to travel abroad. Today, I give lectures and workshops in more than 18 countries in America and Europe. What a fortune mine is!

What was once a bad thing later became a good thing. Therefore, although I do not wish anyone to go through what I have gone through, I must recognize that each step has been necessary to get to where I am.

Is it easy for you to find learning in difficult times? Are you able to feel thankful even for those moments of difficulty? Maybe it's worth thinking a little more like Buddha.

Give your "review" to this great thinker on the following scale. How much do you agree with Buddha?

From his writings, it can be inferred that for *Plato (427 BC - 347 BC)*, happiness consists in ensuring that those things that lead us to that much-desired emotion depend only on ourselves. "The man who makes everything that leads to happiness depend upon himself, and not upon other men, has adopted the best plan for living happily." Will this be a declaration of renouncing what we cannot control? Is it an invitation to total acceptance of our reality? Is it necessary to live without stress to be happy?

In the most recent investigation of the American Psychological Association (APA) in the report "Stress in America 2020: A National Mental Health Crisis" (American Psychological Association, 2020), it was found that **nine out of ten visits to the doctor are related to stress. What a fact!**

It is no news to anyone that most of us experience high levels of stress, and our body begins to feel the ravages of it. Headaches, cervical or lumbar contractures, colitis, gastritis, high blood pressure, diabetes and even heart attacks result from high levels of cortisol and adrenaline in our body.

As if this was not enough, we receive daily messages that push us to desire and achieve more. "You can do it!", "you are capable of anything!", "You can do that and more, more, MORE!" are just some of the many phrases that haunt the executive world today, not to mention the great marketing that pushes us to systematically want more and, at the same time, throw away what we have used for some time, even though it still works. Even though it's new.

> At this moment, I am reminded of a segment of the beautiful essay The Paradox of Our Age (Moorehead, 1995). The author of these words, an American pastor, wrote: "... These are days of quick trips, disposable diapers, throw-away morality, one-night stands, overweight bodies, and pills that do everything from cheer to quiet,

> to kill. It is a time when there is much in the show window and nothing in the stockroom. A time when technology can bring this letter to you, and a time when you can choose either to share this insight or just to hit delete..."

Always wanting more, and being frequently bombarded with the need to acquire, buy and possess, only add to the already large number of goals, objectives and expectations that we as humans place on ourselves. We are overstimulated!

The Gallup company tells us that most voluntary resignations are due to a bad relationship with the immediate supervisor (Robison, 2008). So, having a bad boss, a poor work environment, physical pain, negative emotions, and a high work overload make it difficult to think we can handle everything. Stress does its thing unless we learn from the teacher Stephen Covey (2020) and his circles of influence. With this useful tool, we can identify the difference between what we can control and influence and what we can dream about and hope for.

For example, a customer service agent of a retail company can only control how he treats his customers. With his emotional intelligence, he can influence how customers respond, but that does not guarantee that all customers of that store will leave satisfied and happy. Some of them could have problems that exceed the scope and control of the store manager, so he will only sometimes be able to influence their character or adverse reactions.

This manager might be stressed out by wanting all the customers to leave the store happy when that is outside his control. Unfortunately, some factors contributing to a customer's happiness have nothing to do with what the customer service agent, the manager or even the company owner can offer.

According to Plato, this manager would benefit if he only focused on what he can control and made his happiness depend only on how he treats customers and not on some other factor that arises, such as how they respond.

Give your "review" to this great thinker on the following scale. How much do you agree with Plato?

For *Aristotle*, a follower of *Plato* (350 years BC), ***eudaimonia*** (good fortune or life) is the result of leading a virtuous life and good fortune (Aristotle, 2001). From this, we can infer that happiness depends partially on ourselves, based on our virtues, and, on the other hand, it also requires a touch of good luck or fortune.

The possibility that some people are born with a "lucky star," and others are born "under a bad sign" frequently appears in Greek culture. Do you think this is so? How much does your happiness depend on luck? Do you know anyone who seems like they were born to be happy?

Give your "review" to this great thinker on the following scale. How much do you agree with Aristotle?

From *Seneca's* words (4 BC- 65 AD), we learn that life's greater blessings are found within the same human being, so they are always within our reach. He describes that **the philosopher is content with what he has without desiring what he does not possess** (Veyne, 1995). Will it be happiness to have a conformist approach to life?

Could it be that not wanting anything is having everything, or is there nothing more to want when you have everything? *Seneca* tells us that the absence of desire allows us access to happiness, being content with what we have, finding joy in what we already own and not desiring things that do not yet belong to us. What do you think?

Give your "review" to this great thinker on the following scale. How much do you agree with Seneca?

Saint Thomas Aquinas (1225-1274), in his research on happiness, tells us that "**the ultimate goal of men cannot consist in wealth, nor honours, nor pleasures, nor the health and pleasures of the body, nor the goods of the soul, nor in the man himself.**" Then, he supports this claim with seven arguments (Thomas Aquinas, 1988). If this is true, then where is happiness? Is it even achievable in this realm? It makes you wonder, right?

At the beginning of 2009, I decided to conduct a series of interviews with people 75 years old or older. The purpose of these interviews was to know the different perspectives each had regarding life, happiness and, of course, old age.

This is how I interviewed people from the most diverse fields, some of whom awaited death bedridden while others continued to run marathons, some surrounded by family members and others who spent their days in solitude. I interviewed 75 people of different religions and beliefs, and that's how I came across the rabbi.

Well over 80 years and known for being one of the pioneers of the Jewish community in northern Mexico, the rabbi proudly welcomed me into his home. First, he invited me to taste a delicious sweet. Then, even though it was nine o'clock in the morning, he insisted that we have some Manischewitz wine. I had not had breakfast, and you can imagine the result. What an interview!

"Drink a little," he said while pointing to the glass of sweet wine he had served me. I asked him about love, life and happiness between sip and sip, and when he answered, he took me by the hand to see the photographs that had great personalities of that time. He could be seen both with governors, artists, athletes and presidents. He even mentioned that one of the main squares in the city's center would bear his name as soon as he died. Recognition was his happiness!

A few days later, I interviewed the president of the Church of Jesus Christ of Latter-day Saints (commonly called Mormons). He welcomed me at his house and kindly answered my questions. I asked about life, love and happiness. He responded modestly and avoided using "pride" in his vocabulary, even asking me to rephrase questions when "pride" was present.

"What makes you proud?" I asked. "I prefer to answer what makes me happy. Is that okay?" he answered, giving me a list of experiences with other human beings from his family or community. I believe he found happiness in humility, a completely opposite definition of happiness to what the rabbi had found. What do you think? Should we forget about the accolades and pleasures of life? Should we make them part of our happiness? Where is the balance? Let's keep learning!

Give your "review" to this great thinker on the following scale. How much do you agree with Thomas Aquinas?

From the great *Immanuel Kant* (1724-1804), we can learn that happiness, more than a desire, is an obligation, a duty of the human being. Kant tells us that happiness does not depend on anyone but ourselves and that we must find it. **Would you agree that happiness is your only and most important focus?** Should one indulge in pleasures? Would it be worth defining the term first before indulging in your search? Certainly tempting!

Give your "review" to this great thinker on the following scale. How much do you agree with Kant?

On the other hand, *John Stuart Mill* (1806-1873) invites us to seek what gives us pleasure and to stay away from everything that causes us pain (utilitarianism). It sounds logical until some people, relationships, and social contexts are harmful or painful. Should we stay away from those people?

As time passes and I get older, I gave up on some "friends" because of the negative emotions they brought into my life. So, in a way, I prefer to keep close to me, only those who feed my spirit and help me grow in an environment of well-being.

Pessimists, criticizers, gossip, revengeful liars and thugs are quickly removed from my closest circle of friends. I'm not talking about those who give constructive feedback; I'm referring to those who only complain and complain without making changes. Some are kept as acquaintances, but I don't spend much time interacting with them. Although I previously wanted to keep them close, hoping they would change their way of being, **I choose my well-being and emotional peace over all things today.**

It can be challenging to maintain a close circle of positive people. Sometimes it isn't easy to get away from those who are close relatives, even if their behaviours' or words hurt us (I, for instance, have a relative who always has a "tragedy" to share, her happiness is pain and sadness. Unfortunately, it is more common than you think!). However, maintaining peace and emotional well-being is essential for me. To provide peace, I must first cultivate it within me.

In this sense, what things or people would you give up to be happy? Is this approach selfish? Should we be forced to live with all people, even if they hurt us?

Give your "review" to this great thinker on the following scale. How much do you agree with *John Stuart*?

From *Henry David Thoreau's* (1817-1862) famous work Walden, we can learn his concept of happiness in the following analogy: "**Happiness is like a butterfly, the more you chase it, the more it will evade you, but if you turn your attention to other things around you, it will gently come and sit on your shoulder**." (Thoreau, 2005). If true, the key would be to stop trying so hard to be happy and get busy with something else. Quite the opposite of what Kant suggested!

I love motorcycle trips. In the city where I live (Niagara Falls, ON), motorcycle rides are restricted to good weather, which occurs between May and September, months in which we see the maple trees bloom and turn green until the fall season begins and, with it, the yellow, red and sienna colours that paint the scene.

People often ask me what I enjoy most about riding a motorcycle. The answer is short and straightforward: inside my helmet, there is peace.

Despite being on a busy highway, despite riding with other motorcyclists, even in the middle of a storm, inside my helmet, there is peace.

That peace allows me to find enough tranquillity for the butterfly of happiness to perch on my soul, sometimes at more than 100 km/h, while in others leaning back on the motorcycle while parked and enjoying the scenery. Inside my helmet, there is peace!

A ride around Niagara river, Niagara Falls, ON

Whenever I find peace in these rides, I do as Henry David Thoreau, ride enjoying the road and the scenery, and the butterfly lands on my shoulders. (fastest butterfly in town)

What do you think? Do you believe that happiness comes when you take a break? If so, how many breaks have you taken lately?

Give your "review" to this great thinker on the following scale. How much do you agree with Thoreau?

From the much-mentioned *Friedrich Nietzsche* (1844-1900), we can infer that happiness is only achieved by overcoming adversity. It appears as the moment in which we feel powerful and full of vitality.

If so, does happiness depend on how many problems you have overcome? Do those who do not face serious problems cannot be happy? This reminds me of a friend I used to chat with while practicing martial arts. He would tell me, "No pain, no gain."

Many believe that tasting the bitter galls of suffering is necessary to achieve happiness. What do you think? Could only those people who go through difficult situations enjoy happiness?

Give your "review" to this great thinker on the following scale. How much do you agree with *Nietzsche*?

José Ortega y Gasset (1883-1955) somehow relates happiness to the time we invest in those activities that produce a state of passion in us. Passion! (Deep sigh!)

Have you ever worked so focused that you ended up forgetting lunchtime? Have you taken on a task that makes you forget everything, even taking a bio-break? (Nice way of saying going to the washroom.) Indeed, you were then living your passion, that state that Dr. Robert Vallerand (Vallerand, 2010) describes as **the strong inclination towards an activity that the person loves, considers important and to which they dedicate significant amounts of time and energy. The moment in which everything flows, we are connected with our abilities and talent; moments in which time passes differently, and we achieve our maximum potential. The flow!** (Deep sigh again!)

The state of passion is typically achieved when performing tasks we enjoy. When we use our character strengths (see VIA test) to perform activities throughout the day, the state of passion that allows us to enjoy what we do occurs much more frequently. Will that be happiness? How much do you enjoy what you do?

Give your "review" to this great thinker on the following scale. How much do you agree with *Ortega y Gasset*?

But we have one more author, and by the way, on this copy of the book is the most important of them all: ______________________ (*your name goes here*); you, my reader, and your definition of happiness, which can be completely different from any of the previous ones or a combination of them.

What definition of happiness seems more akin to you? Why? (You can combine two or more authors in your answer.)

For this book, and following the philosophy of the *Emotional Paycheck Institute of Canada®*, happiness depends on us and the care we give to each of the six categories of well-being. This is, of course, besides influencing factors related to good fortune. **We can do the hard work and hope for a piece of good luck; that always helps!**

Now that you have a better understanding of the high dynamism that the definition of happiness implies, you'll understand that the *subjectivity* of the topic is such that it is practically impossible to measure it in someone other than ourselves. After all, the person in front of you might have a completely different definition of happiness. And for sure, it's going to change!

Now that we have established that happiness cannot be measured in someone else let's look at how that feeling of happiness is generated in our brains.

Did you know there is a group of hormones called the Fantastic 4 of Happiness? Let's get to know about them!

3

The Fantastic 4 of happiness

Plus one

Do you remember falling in love? The moment when that special someone appeared in your life, that person that makes you (or made you) feel young again when you see them. No matter what the calendar says, you are young. That beautiful feeling overwhelms you with strong energy and makes you feel relaxed. Emotions take over you, making you feel connected, while the simplest jokes bring you happiness and laughter. When the four hormones of happiness are abundant in your body, you are in love! Later in life, one gets married, and we never see them together again (I'm just kidding!).

The hormones of happiness are at our disposal in multiple ways. Although they indeed abound when falling in love, accessing them through other mechanisms is also possible. Keep reading!

Dopamine, oxytocin, endorphins, serotonin and melatonin are necessary to balance enjoyment and well-being. If you read carefully and notice details, you have already noticed five. This is because I added one more hormone to the recognized list. Find out which one I've added!

Dopamine appears when we smile, enjoy a moment, and laugh out loud. **How long has it been since you laughed until your stomach hurts?** It is crucial to stay close to those people who make us laugh. And although the workplace must maintain a certain formality, we must also allow spaces for enjoyment and laughter. I'm sure you remember a coworker who makes you laugh with their witticisms.

Also, dopamine is released upon task completion, generating a sense of achievement. When we compile a list of tasks at the start of the day and progressively mark them off as we work through the day, the satisfaction derived from this process triggers the dopamine release in our brains.

Unfortunately, most of us set ambitious goals and have little access to that feeling of accomplishment. Establishing attainable and realistic tasks is important to enhance your chances of experiencing contentment. By creating a list of objectives that can be accomplished within your working hours, you are setting yourself up for success. As you steadily complete each task, the arrival of dopamine will contribute to an improved sense of well-being. Therefore, after a demanding day at work, you will have a much greater opportunity to feel satisfied.

Exercise: How would you like to promote dopamine in your life? What would you do to increase the amount of this hormone in your system?

Do you remember the last time you hugged someone you loved? Perhaps you have felt a tickling sensation in your chest that invited you to squeeze that person a little tighter, led you to hold the hug for a little longer, or even let out a smile and a sigh while you continued hugging them. This is the work of oxytocin, also known as the cuddle hormone.

When your boss wants to hug you to release oxytocin.

Certainly, hugging is generally not considered appropriate in a professional setting. However, in some instances, we may form friendships with colleagues that lead to more casual expressions of connection, like handshakes, maintaining eye contact, sharing smiles, and occasionally even hugging. In certain workplaces, there might be a pet, typically a dog or a cat, present to trigger oxytocin, and it's worth noting that hugging a pet can elicit a similar effect as hugging another person.

Exercise: How would you like to promote oxytocin in your life? What would you do to increase the amount of this hormone in your system? How do you encourage social interaction with other human beings?

What is your favourite song? A song that cheers you up and, before you realize it, makes you shake your head to its rhythm. Serotonin is invading your body thanks to the power of music, which leads us to a change in our state of mind. Friedrich Nietzsche, who often expressed his pessimistic views about life, mentioned that life without music would be a mistake. It is that powerful!

I often recommend my patients review the music they listen to carefully. Accessing melodies and songs that cause enjoyment, improve our mood, and make us feel good, is essential for our well-being. So, take care of your playlist!

While dopamine is associated with individual task completion and a sense of personal accomplishment, serotonin plays a crucial role in group goals, team efforts, and connection with others while working towards a shared objective.

When we engage in collaborative projects or contribute to a team effort, serotonin levels can increase. This neurotransmitter is associated with well-being, satisfaction, and belonging. It helps foster positive social interactions and a sense of camaraderie among team members.

Furthermore, the perception of connection to other humans and the shared pursuit of a greater goal can trigger serotonin release. When we connect to a larger purpose and work together towards a meaningful objective, serotonin levels may rise, creating a sense of fulfillment and happiness.

So, while dopamine is linked to personal achievements, serotonin highlights the importance of teamwork, shared goals, and human connection in enhancing our overall well-being and satisfaction.

Exercise: How would you like to promote serotonin in your life? What would you do to increase the amount of this hormone in your system? When was the last time you listened to good music?

Besides its close connection to music, there are other ways to increase your serotonin levels. A recent study correlates the amount of serotonin with the collective goals we pursue. Personal goals are linked to dopamine, while collective goals are related to serotonin. Both hormones are essential; making a daily list of your goals will help you increase dopamine levels while sharing goals with a group of people will trigger your serotonin. Isn't that awesome?

Endorphins appear after a session of exercise. But fear not: you won't have to become the next Olympian to feel their effects. It is enough to increase the heart rate to generate the endorphins that make us feel good. As you know, exercise is essential to maintain physical and mental health.

Exercise: How would you like to promote endorphins in your

life? What would you do to increase the amount of this hormone in your system? When was the last time you exercised?

So far, we have four hormones, and although the list often ends there, I have decided to add a hormone that requires a lot of attention lately. Unfortunately, it's frequently overlooked!

How long has it been since you woke up wanting to "eat the world"? How long have you not slept well? I often hear how executives compete to see who got the least sleep. While one declares that he went to sleep after midnight, another wants to beat him by saying he has not slept. They are definitely in the wrong competition. I would rather compete to see who slept more and better, don't you agree?

Melatonin appears to control our sleep cycle. It is an important hormone that allows us to sleep soundly at the right time. It invites us to have a restful sleep and, thus, be able to approach the next day with new energy.

That is why I always add it as a fantastic of happiness. That makes them five!

Exercise: How would you like to promote melatonin in your life? What would you do to increase the amount of this hormone in your system?

> In conclusion: we need more laughter, good music, exercise, personal and team goals, hugging and sleep; all of them within our reach without the need for a budget; all of them frequently ignored by executives who chase more money, thinking that it will provide them with the wellbeing they forget to enjoy while pursuing the economic salary. The unfortunate "rat race."

What happens when the hormones of happiness are not present? Their antithesis appears; the stress hormones arise. In the adrenal gland, just above our kidneys, two hormones are secreted when we are under stress: adrenaline and cortisol.

Think about when you were walking down the street and out of nowhere, a barking dog appeared, or a car alarm went off. You jumped much faster and higher than you usually would, ran a lot quicker, and a few seconds later, you felt like your strength was leaving you, maybe even felt like you were fainting. These are the effects of cortisol and adrenaline!

Cortisol is critical to activate the mechanism that allows us to stay alive, the survival "fight or flight" mechanism, which leads us to make fundamental decisions in dangerous situations.

Accompanied by cortisol comes adrenaline, which gives us enough energy to achieve our chosen mission, whether fighting as hard as the most skilled boxer or running as fast as the fastest athlete. You are strong, fast, and almost invincible—at least for a few seconds while the adrenaline lasts.

While this mechanism has evolutionarily allowed the survival of the human being, if it stays active for long periods of time, it may lead us to develop some stress-related diseases. As previously remarked, nine out of ten medical consultations concern stress-related issues. Adrenaline and cortisol have become our enemies, as they are present daily at work, and lately, we work every day.

Thanks to the smartphone, we find ourselves hyper-connected. Thanks to the home office, we start working from bed and even from the bathroom. There is no rest, no disconnection, and stress is always present, so cortisol does its thing.

It is time to reduce cortisol levels and start having a much more pleasant life. But how to achieve this? Here are some techniques that health professionals suggest to reduce cortisol levels.

- **Keep an eye on sleep patterns**: Seven to eight hours of quality sleep each night is the gold standard for optimal health and makes for a powerful cortisol reducer. If you need more rest, try an earlier bedtime. If you can only fall asleep late at night, try dimming the lights and turning off phones, computers, and televisions at least an hour before bed.

- **Be careful with caffeine**: I know this one is going to be hard for many to take in, but yes, caffeine increases cortisol. Of course, you do not have to stop drinking your morning cup of coffee. Still, if you are a coffee lover or enjoy drinking any other caffeinated beverage, you should consider reducing coffee cups throughout the day and avoiding it after 2 pm. This will dramatically help your sleep cycles.

- **Outdoor Activity**: Fresh air and sunlight are the Zen masters: they have a way of clearing the mind that results in lower cortisol levels. Start spending some time in nature and admire the beauty of mother earth. Whether sitting on a park bench, walking down a trail, or just strolling your neighbourhood streets, outdoor activities remind us that we are part of a whole and naturally relax the body.

- **Move your body**: You need exercise to have a strong and toned body, but some movement also does wonders for your mind. Exercise is a significant player on the list of what lowers cortisol. Your brain releases endorphins that make you feel good when you exercise, and research has shown substantial benefits from the impact of endorphins on cortisol levels (Taylor T., 1983).

As we can see, cortisol can be controlled with simple activities that do not require any investment. So, what do you plan to do to reduce cortisol levels?

Let's continue our journey to ignite the bonfire of well-being that will allow the flame of happiness to appear.

The presence of all the happiness-related hormones is often heightened during the experience of love. However, it is ironic that after getting married, we often find ourselves unable to witness the simultaneous occurrence of these hormones. We may attribute this to the commonly heard phrase, "It's not you, it's me," and indeed, we may be right. It is our responsibility to actively nurture and promote the production of these hormones to maintain and enhance our happiness levels.

Dr. Leal

4

The bonfire of wellbeing

WHAT'S THAT?

I have always had a special admiration for firefighters. They run towards danger while everyone else is running from it. The heavy equipment and machinery they carry have always caught my attention. At some point, I thought about registering as a volunteer firefighter. I even took basic training despite a constant scolding from my father, who was adamantly opposed to the idea.

During my training, I learnt about the triangle of fire: oxygen, heat and fuel. The fire goes out if any of the three is absent. Thanks to this triangle, we now know that there is more than one way to extinguish a fire:

- Limiting the amount of oxygen,
- Reducing the heat source,
- Waiting for the fuel to run out.

But we don't always want the fire to go out. Fire is a faithful companion in the history of modern humankind. It is impossible to think of a modern society without access to fire. An example of this is the barbecue campfire that, for millennia, has gathered human beings around the fire, whether ceremonially or for nourishment. Fire is always present in fables, tales, legends, and universal mythology.

In more modern times, we mainly use fire to cook. In my case, I love a good barbecue in my backyard. If we want to light a fire to cook a barbecue, we must use good firewood, that is, good fuel. At the same time, it is necessary to apply enough heat to start the fire. We do this regularly with a match (or several if you are inexperienced), and, of course, we must feed the fire with enough air to increase the oxygen so its flames are fanned. When the three elements of fire are present, we can light the fire and enjoy a good barbecue.

Suppose any elements (fire, oxygen or fuel) were in poor condition. In that case, it would be more challenging to light the fire; it would not be impossible, but it would certainly not be that easy. Something similar happens in the bonfire of well-being. It requires all the necessary elements to ignite well-being in ourselves and facilitate the appearance of the flame of happiness. If one of those elements is weak, lighting the flame will be more difficult. If they are absent, the campfire will be extinguished, and their well-being will be gone.

All the elements are important to the bonfire of well-being, but humans must combine them to light their flame of happiness. Well-being is having all the elements available. Happiness is deciding to light them on.

Our wellness bonfire requires six elements, and at the Emotional Paycheck Institute, we call them wellness categories. Although these categories/elements of the bonfire are the same for everyone, we will all have our way of starting a wellness bonfire. Therefore, we cannot compare our bonfire with someone else's, even if we have the same elements or categories.

The presence or absence of each well-being category necessary to start our bonfire is subjective. No one can tell you how low or high any of your elements needs to be, much less can they decide if that is good or bad. Your rating is entirely subjective: it is based only on what you feel, and you are its only judge and witness. It's your life. It's your campfire!

Due to their subjectivity, we call each element to light the bonfire of well-being categories of the subjective perception of wellbeing. (SPW)

Each of the categories of the SPW necessary to start the bonfire of wellbeing generates in your body the hormones that we mentioned in the fantastic of happiness and promotes the emotions required for wellbeing and happiness.

Ready to review the necessary items for the bonfire of wellness? Let's clarify: Well-being does not always depend on you; happiness does. Let me explain!

Well-being does not always depend on you. Happiness does

A certain saying goes: "Nobody can make you happy if you don't want to be," and I couldn't agree more. Happiness is an emotional state generated when the hormones mentioned above appear. Throughout history, many have managed to create forms of happiness, even in the most challenging situations we can imagine, while other human beings who seem to "have it all" end up taking their own lives or plunging into addictions. Why?

Because happiness depends on oneself and is only facilitated through well-being, it means having all the elements of happiness available to you. Happiness is deciding to turn them on. Let me tell you a very personal story!

I'm in Port-au-Prince. It's the month of January, just a few days after the strongest earthquake Haiti has experienced in recent history.

Thousands of houses are completely destroyed. Also, the most affluent residential area (Petion-Ville) is devastated. Even the presidential house is split in half. Everything is chaos, and as I walk the streets, I see how the bodies of the fatalities are burned on the corners while just a few meters ahead, some children are playing ball. This was just one of the thousands of dystopic scenes I remember from that mission.

During the first hours of the morning, I arrive at SONAPI, an industrial park in the free trade zone of Haiti that has been conditioned to receive foreign volunteers. I come hand in hand with my friend Ramón Molina, a soldier and volunteer from the Dominican Republic whom I met a few years ago whilst training with the police in Mexico.

We settled in a field hospital some Dominicans built to provide primary medical care to the locals. The clinic was later administered by the organization Médecins du Mond.

My main goal as a volunteer is to provide psychological care to patients still in shock, but as is often the case, I do a bit of everything. I organize my consultations while there is a water shortage and the most essential resources are scarce. We do not even have a fixed place to hold our sessions; I improvised two blocks as chairs and placed them under the shade of a tree. Only half a litre of water must be consumed by the volunteers daily. We are completely dehydrated!

Patients arrive in large numbers, many of them with injuries that exceed the healing materials we have in the hospital. Among them is a woman in her thirties who declares that her son and husband died in the earthquake a few days ago.

That's not all. This woman is facing the loss of her relatives in the collapse of her house, and she has also arrived with multiple leg injuries. She was trapped in a semi-collapsed market where she went looking for something to eat. She entered a semi-destroyed building, and one of the walls tumbled, trapping both extremities at knee level. The doctor thinks that the only solution to save her life is to amputate them. What a tragedy!

Nadege is just one of the hundreds of cases I saw firsthand in that humanitarian rescue mission. Thousands of people were left helpless, homeless, looking for their relatives. If there are ever reasons to be sad, they were all reunited in Haiti.

Haiti, 2010

After losing her legs in surgery, Nadege was moved into a small 4m x 4m tent donated by Rotary International®. A few hours passed, and she woke up extremely upset by what had happened.

She blamed me, blamed the doctor, and even cursed everyone who entered her room, which was especially awkward since she was in the same room as two other patients who required daily visits.

My morning routine included visiting the patients in their rooms. Inside each tent, three small mats were placed on the floor in a horseshoe shape, labelled A, B, and C clockwise. I will never forget that Nadege was at the C just to the right when I entered the room.

She tried everything—she threw feces at me, tried to prick me with a used syringe, and even cast a voodoo spell so that I would suffer as she suffered. She was distraught by what was happening and vented her fury on me and other volunteers.

The days passed, and I continued to visit my patients, always taking care of my interaction and closeness with Nadege, who became quieter as the weeks passed.

One morning, she wouldn't even make eye contact with me. Instead, she was focused on looking at the room's ceiling while I was chatting with the other patients, and the vibe in the room felt different. I began to check her hands without her realizing it. I tried to identify if it was another plan to hurt me, but this time her hands were in plain sight, and her gaze was lost on the white vinyl of the tent's ceiling.

I approached the exit, still surrounded by this strange silence. Nadege always cursed and threw objects at me with annoyance when she saw me. However, it was different now, so I left the room only to return in less than two seconds.

"Ou bien?" (Are you okay?) I asked with some curiosity. "Mewn enkyete!" (I'm worried), she replied. Then, I entered her tent again to begin a long conversation about her future and what she could do now that she was homeless and had lost her legs. For the first time, we discussed something that could be modified: the future!

Nadege was surprised that I wanted to help her after everything she had done against me. Still, I helped her understand that she was upset with herself and her circumstances. I understood that her anger was not against me, although I have to admit that the blows hurt a lot ("Ou se yon bon boxer" (you have a boxer's arm), I told her while I was rubbing my arm. (Nadege laughed).

We chatted long through the days, and she even performed a ritual to lift the curses she had placed on me. It was a nice gift that I always keep in my mind.

What had changed? Why did Nadege go from being upset to wishing me good fortune? She still had no legs, and her relatives would never see her again. She hadn't changed anything on the outside, but she had changed everything on the inside. Even though the conditions for Nadege's welfare remained the same, she had changed, taking advantage of the little support available to her at the time. She gathered the available well-being items and started working on igniting them again. A new bonfire was born, good for Nadege!

Well-being has to do with the conditions surrounding us, which can be scarce or abundant. Still, they can only be taken advantage of when the individual focuses on them positively. Well-being does not depend entirely on you, but happiness does.

Of course, it is easier to be happy if our well-being categories are properly balanced. However, even if we have all the well-being categories in abundance, we can only be happy if we decide to be happy.

Happiness is a decision. As such, it cannot be measured precisely. It is only experienced by those who promote it in their lives. On the other hand, well-being can be consciously measured, promoted, controlled and even improved. I insist that happiness cannot be measured, but well-being can.

So, what are these categories of well-being? How can we generate an environment in which the categories of well-being are present and properly balanced? Keep reading!

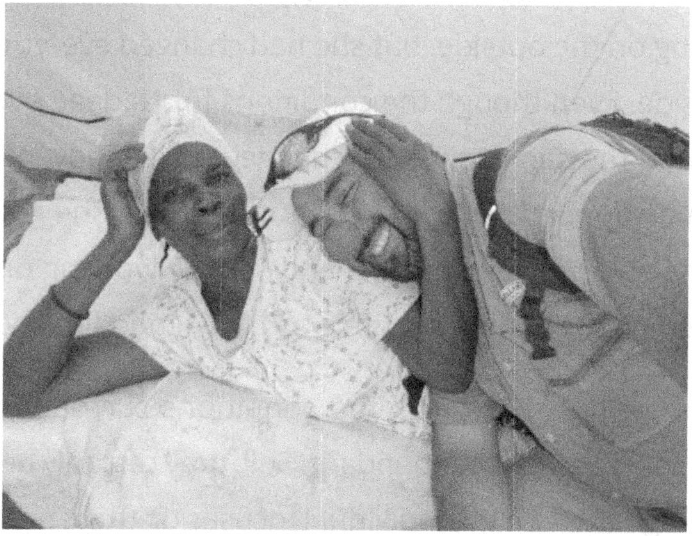

Haiti 2010

5

Your bonfire elements

Gathering the best wood

As we have discussed, happiness cannot be measured due to its dynamic nature. The good news is well-being can. Happiness and wellness are not the same, but they are very much connected!

For this analysis, well-being is that state of personal satisfaction and comfort that facilitates the appearance of emotions of happiness and is related to all aspects that surround the human being.

Well-being is having all the necessary elements to be able to light that bonfire we have talked about. It is the platform on which happiness can be present much more frequently. If you have these elements, you will have much easier and more constant access to satisfaction.

Well-being includes those physical, emotional, financial, spiritual, social and community aspects necessary to enjoy a dignified and potentially happy life. This life can constantly and consistently generate the dopamine, serotonin, endorphins and oxytocin required for the emotions connected to happiness.

Companies, political parties, governments across the globe, business leaders, parents and teachers, and every conscious adult should promote the different categories of well-being in their environments since this facilitates the appearance of happiness in its various forms.

Can you increase your well-being? Of course! The good news is it often doesn't take much work to improve each category. On many occasions (maybe more than you would think), we find how minor adjustments allow great results in this area. Sometimes, it only takes us to be aware of the importance of certain things within our reach, but we tend to forget to stimulate. Interesting!

How long will it take me to increase my well-being? In the same way that happiness is unique to each person, the time you will see results in each well-being category varies from person to person. However, most people will be able to perceive positive changes after two weeks (Passmore et al., 2017), while it could take a little longer for others. But don't worry too much about it. Everyone has their own formula and time to get the bonfire started!

Where does this well-being come from? Well-being comes from both external and internal sources, depending on the type of category we are referring to. Sometimes it will depend on external factors, such as our relationships with other people or our environment. Meanwhile, on other occasions, it will be more of an introspection exercise in which we must change how we interpret the situations around us.

What are the categories of the subjective perception of well-being? Let's start by looking at the name:

"Category" refers to the subdivision of the concept of well-being into the different aspects that compose it.

"Subjective" refers to the interpretation that the human being makes of that reality and its environment. It is subject to its filters and can differ for each person.

"Perception" is what a human being receives as an interpretation of their environment.

"Wellbeing" is a term we have already defined in this section as that state of personal satisfaction and comfort which facilitates the appearance of happiness.

So, when referring to the categories of the subjective perception of well-being, we are talking about that categorization (subdivision) of the different aspects that a human being perceives and that provide comfort in their life. At the institute, we call them *SPW categories* (Subjective Perception of Wellness) because I am from Monterrey, and I like to save words.

Positive psychology interventions to increase self-reported well-being and decrease depressive symptoms are becoming increasingly popular (et al., 2009). There is evidence of its substantially positive effects (Woodworth et al., 2013); however, like all developing science, its detractors consider it ineffective (Mongrain et al., 2012). The truth is that positive psychology and the categories of the SPW gain more followers daily and are presented as an excellent way to measure well-being at a personal and business level.

As we analyze each category of the subjective perception of well-being (SPW), I invite you to explore how these are currently present in your personal and work life. Likewise, you will be able to identify which specific activities you should incorporate in each of these categories to increase the chances of happiness appearing both at a work and personal level. Here we go!

Note: When understanding the essential elements of well-being, it's important to note that various lists exist, each offering its unique perspective. Some sources, such as the book "Wellbeing" and others, outline five fundamental elements that contribute to overall well-being. On the other hand, sources like PMC-NCBI mention a comprehensive framework of eight mutually interdependent dimensions. However, this book will focus on the six elements identified by the author and director of the Emotional Paycheck Institute. By exploring and analyzing these specific elements, we aim to understand better the factors contributing to our emotional well-being and overall satisfaction in life.

Social SPW

Charles is a project leader who works in a technology company, has certifications in project management and agile methodologies and has recently achieved the "scrum master" degree, which places him far ahead of other project leaders in the company. Without a doubt, Carlos is extraordinarily qualified.

Carlos's boss has an autocratic leadership style of "no news, good news"; the boss only gives feedback when things go wrong. There is no recognition or positive feedback.

Carlos is unsure about the quality of his work, he does not know if his boss notices his efforts, and although he is not certified in the emotional paycheck, Carlos feels that he is not adequately recognized.

Sarah is the mother of two children. She works as an executive in a bank in Ecuador. With her salary, she supports her mother, who helps with the children at home.

Sarah's children have already grown up and are going through their teenage stage; sometimes, they don't come home to sleep, they rarely hug her, and she doesn't remember the last time they said: "thank you." Sarah feels unmotivated and questions whether she has been a good mother.

Carlos and Sarah lack recognition, appreciation and affection that have yet to be covered, which is why their category of the Social SPW needs some work.

The social category of well-being connects us with what brings positive emotions, a feeling of connection with other human beings, and the possibility that what we do is appreciated by the people around us.

It is time for you to evaluate, in your particular case, the quantity and quality of the love, respect, recognition and appreciation you receive from the people around you, whether at work or home.

To help you analyze this category more specifically, I invite you to answer the following questions.

Personal social category: The quantity and quality of love, appreciation, respect and affection you perceive from your family and close friends.

Work social category: The recognition and appreciation you receive from your work environment (boss, colleagues, clients, and community).

Support questions:

- How valued do you feel in your job right now?
- How valued do you feel by your family right now?
- How many expressions of appreciation and respect do you receive in your work?
- How many tokens of appreciation and respect do you receive from your family?
- How much love do you perceive towards yourself

from your work environment?

- How much love do you perceive towards yourself from your family?
- With your answers, you should be able to evaluate the category of the PSB both in your personal and work life.

Community SPW

A few days ago, while visiting friends for Thanksgiving, I saw how one of the family's grandparents, an (approximately) 85-year-old man, was sitting in a chair near the kitchen while the rest of the family shared the main table.

Each relative who arrived showed great appreciation for Grandpa, most brought him a gift, and all showed affection. Surely, the category of the subjective perception of the grandpa's social well-being was quite nourished. However, as soon as they greeted the grandfather, they were ready to start a conversation with someone else. Amid all the people of his family, Grandpa was alone!

Maybe because he was a little deaf, maybe because he had no knowledge of current affairs, or maybe because he was the only one without a smartphone, nobody chatted with Grandpa. It was like he didn't belong.

I remember when I first arrived in Canada in 2010. I would go to work meetings and, in each session, I would connect with potential new friends; however, when the weekend arrived, I would find myself alone. From Monday to Friday, I had work, but on the weekends, my phone did not ring at all. I felt that clients and suppliers appreciated me, and my social status felt satisfied in this new country, but when the weekend arrived, I felt that I did not belong.

Grandpa and I suffered from the same problem: A low rating from the Community SPW!

Subjective perception of personal community wellbeing category: Quantity and quality of bonds and emotional connections with other people within the personal circle (friends, family, hobby groups, etc.).

Subjective perception of work community wellbeing category: Quantity and quality of friendships within the work environment (friends in other departments, feeling of holistic impact, etc.)

To help you analyze this category more specifically, I invite you to answer the following questions.

Support questions:

On a professional level:

How much do you perceive you impact your company through your actions?

How easily do you identify how you contribute to other departments, areas, or projects in the organization?

How connected do you feel about the outcome of the company you work for?

How many of your personal friends also work in the company?

Do you feel like an important part of your work community?

On a personal level:

How connected do you feel with other family members?

How many groups of friends or relatives do you belong to?

These are just some questions that will help you evaluate the quality of your community's well-being.

Career SPW

Ramiro is an IT professional working for a small company in Guadalajara, Mexico company. He has a good salary and the recognition of his colleagues; he is the owner's right-hand man, and in general, Ramiro knows that he holds the electronic keys to the company. His expertise in networking and software development led him to develop an inventory control system that adjusts to business needs. As of today, he is the only one who fully understands the system. He is a fundamental piece for the proper functioning of the manufacturing company he works for. His boss, Rogelio, involves him in all decisions and has provided him with several financial incentives besides his salary. Despite this, Rogelio notices that Ramiro has been somewhat demotivated lately, which concerns him, but there isn't much he can do. Ramiro needs growth that the company cannot fulfill and is ready for new challenges. Do you know someone like that?

Most likely, Ramiro will eventually resign from his job. He might even accept a position that pays slightly less as long as there is the possibility of learning new things and advancing to higher levels. That's how powerful career well-being is.

On more than one occasion, I have seen professionals quit well-paying jobs because they have no professional future. In some cases, like Ramiro's, the next position would be becoming the company's owner, which won't happen. In other cases, executive assistants have a master's degree in business administration and certifications in conflict management, but they are not allowed to make any decisions. Applying our talents, character strengths, and virtues to benefit the organization is essential to experience career well-being.

Being in a situation where you have so many tasks that you experience high levels of stress is just as bad as being in a position where the tasks are so basic that you get bored and feel stagnant. Balance is key! In the Emotional paycheck ambassador certification, we teach a technique called EFC (Equity Flow Chart) that balances the workload across the team of collaborators.

On a personal level, you also have a career: you use your talents to contribute to your family, partner, or group of friends. For me, it is important to be a good father, husband, and son and fulfill my obligations according to the roles I have created for myself as a parent, spouse, and family member. How good of a father am I? How do I perform as a husband? I remember once telling my wife, "I know you are self-sufficient, and I love that about you. You are a successful professional, a very intelligent woman with a lot of energy, but I want you to know that it is important to me to fulfill the role of a husband that I consider appropriate; I need to experience the 3Ps (Provide, Protect, and Proclaim).

“As a husband, I want to **proclaim** that you are my wife, tell my friends, new clients, and people in general that I am married; I am proud to introduce you as my wife, which is important. I am in love and want to tell the world you are my wife.

“Also, I want to **protect** you. I know that you could defend yourself, but in my definition of chivalry and marriage, I love knowing that I can protect you from any danger that may arise, that you are not alone, and that you always have my support.

"Finally, I want to **provide**. It is important to feel that I contribute, cover needs, and provide a house, food, sustenance and other little pleasures that will allow you access to well-being and happiness. I know that you participate and will participate in the financial contribution of our relationship and family. Still, I need to know that I am doing my part, providing and providing well."

In my definition of SPW of Personal Career, my relationship's well-being is defined as how I comply with the proclamation, protection and provision of everything necessary for my family to be well. It is one of the ways how I can perceive if I am a good husband.

To assess the category of the SPW both personally and professionally, answer the following questions:

At a professional level:

- What are your talents, virtues and character strengths?

- What are your technical credentials? Have you acquired new skills recently?
- Do you use this knowledge in your current position?
- Do you have a clear professional growth plan with achievable goals?
- Do you trust that growth will occur within the organization in which you currently work?
- Are the tasks that you perform aligned with your level of training?

On a personal level:

- What are your talents, virtues, and character strengths?
- How do you perform your roles as a parent, partner, son or daughter, sibling, or friend?
- These are some of the questions that will help you gauge the quality of career wellbeing you currently enjoy.

Physical-Emotional SPW

Undoubtedly, this is the most popular category in times of pandemic, where stress levels have reached historic heights, as mentioned before, according to the latest studies by the APA (American Psychology Association). Physical and emotional health are interconnected; we must care for them equally.

Physical care, rest, digital disconnection, spaces for conversation and support, a sense of accomplishment, and good personal relationships within the work environment play an important role in the physical and emotional health of employees in the company. Has your doctor told you that you need to reduce stress levels in your life? Do you suffer from any health challenges related to stress?

To evaluate this category, it is important to know more about the connection between the so-called stress hormone (cortisol) and the physical illnesses we commonly know. Below is a list compiled by R. Morgan Griffin and reviewed by Dr. Joseph Goldberg (Griffin, 2014).

• Constant migraines or headaches: It has been proven that there is a relationship between the occurrence of migraines and headaches and stress levels (Armstrong et al., 2006), and I'm sure this is not surprising to anyone.

• Gastrointestinal problems: Although cortisol does not cause ulcers, it can worsen them. In fact, high-stress levels are related to other gastrointestinal diseases, such as reflux and irritable bowel syndrome (Levenstein, 1998). Do you suffer from any of these?

• Premature aging: I'm sure I have your attention now. Studies conducted with mothers who experienced high-stress levels while caring for children with chronic illnesses showed chromosome-level aging due to stress ranging from seven to seventeen years (Pollack et al., 2018), (Pardon, 2007). Quite a remarkable finding!

• Depression and anxiety: These increasingly common mental health disorders are closely linked to high-stress levels (Griffin, 2014). People with high-stress levels are 80% more likely to suffer from anxiety and depression. And there is little awareness of these in the workplace!

• Diabetes: You may not consider this a stress-related disease; however, high-stress levels affect diabetes in two ways. First, due to the unhealthy habits that can develop when experiencing high-stress levels, and second, high-stress levels appear to be connected to blood sugar levels in the body (Lloyd et al., 2005). The sour taste of stress!

• Obesity: Oh boy! According to recent research, cortisol (the stress hormone) is partly responsible for the additional accumulation of abdominal fat (Björntorp, 2001). That's why I insist my wife that I am not overweight; I'm just highly stressed. I need a massage!

• Heart problems: I think you saw this coming. After mentioning obesity, diabetes, depression, and more, it's natural for the heart to be affected. These problems range from high blood pressure, a common body reaction under stress, to sudden heart attacks due to excessive stress (Chandola et al., 2008).

• Alzheimer's: This terrible disease can develop faster due to high-stress levels, according to studies conducted with some animals (Chong et al., 2005). Almost unbelievable but true!

I am sure that after seeing this list, I already have your attention about the importance of controlling stress levels in our lives. But this category covers an additional topic, the physical subject, one that is often supervised by the area of industrial health and safety.

Some companies provide their collaborators with the necessary equipment to work safely; others do not. Analyze the different ways the company you work for takes care of you. For example, physical care can be easily identified in production areas when the company provides protective equipment such as glasses, gloves, protective shoes, reflective vests, and helmets. Also, in offices, staff can be taken care of by monitoring the quantity and quality of light, air quality, ergonomics with adequate chairs and desks, and even equipping monitors with screen protectors that reduce the impact of blue light on our eyes. These are all signs that the company cares physically for you.

> Employees can receive specific training and equipment to work safely from home.

Now it is time to evaluate the quality of this category in your life.

Support questions:

- Do you have any stress-related illnesses?
- Do you take the initiative to take care of your state of mental

health?

• Do you feel your work directly affects your physical or emotional health? Are you doing something about it?

• How much does your job contribute to your physical and emotional well-being?

• How much do you use your company's physical and emotional health services?

Only one scale is required. The same applies to your personal and work space.

Evaluate and analyze the result!

Emerging research has established a connection between elevated cortisol levels and abdominal fat buildup. A statistic that resonates with me deeply—**I'm not overweight, I'm simply carrying the weight of stress.**

Dr. Leal

Financial SPW

The financial aspect also plays an important role in our happiness, and it is important to consider it as such.

Rosemary has a good job as a call center manager; her company offers her a good salary and some benefits such as grocery vouchers, a canteen with special offers for employees, and commuting benefits. Rosemary is single and still lives at home with her parents, so she can save 90% of what she earns in her current position. However, not everything is peaches and cream for her, as she has some hobbies that are not cheap at all.

There is a casino near her place of work, and she regularly gambles for a few hours. She is a well-known customer of the place and has been known to gamble more than she has won in a month at times. Perhaps driven by the casino's atmosphere, Rosemary also frequently drinks alcoholic beverages, likes to buy designer clothes, and attends every concert in her city. Rosemary has failed to pay her credit card several times, and she has occasionally received calls from the bank at her workplace.

She has a good income but a lousy financial education. She lives with the uncertainty of how much money she owes and whether she can pay it back, and she practically starts each month with a little more debt. She has requested loans from the company she works for several times and is annoyed when they are charged on her payslip. She could be buying a property or saving for retirement, but she can't even cover her most basic expenses. Do you know someone like Rosemary?

The financial SPW is the quality of a person's financial health considering their income, expenses, savings, ability to save and invest, and consumer habits. It's not just about the money they earn but the money they can keep after covering their expenses.

The pursuit of wealth is an ongoing race with no finish line. Even the richest individuals on the planet continue to strive for more money. Moreover, your financial status can be relative, as what may be considered rich to someone in one part of the world might be seen as poor in the eyes of others. The concept of wealth is subjective, much like the definition of happiness. Therefore, we cannot solely measure our financial well-being based on a specific amount of money. Instead, we should consider the balance between our income and expenses and how much we earn and spend to evaluate our financial health.

It's time to measure your Financial SPW:

Support questions:

- How are your finances?
- Does your economic salary allow you to cover your debts and have the capacity to save?
- Do you have so much debt that you need a second or third job to cover your expenses?
- Is your economic situation due to a lack of financial education?

These are some of the questions that will help you assess whether your financial category is in good condition.

Spiritual SPW

Although we mention only five categories of well-being in the corporate environment, there is one more personal level that I'd like to invite you to evaluate: the one that connects you with your beliefs. Unfortunately, we sometimes forget about it because we are immersed in the race to do more, have more, and do everything faster. This category is about the subjective perception of spiritual well-being.

How long has it been since you spent a moment alone? I don't mean that moment when you isolate yourself on the phone watching memes and videos, but a moment when you connect with yourself and answer transcendental questions as the reason or purpose of your life, how you want to be remembered or how you would describe yourself without using titles, age, degrees, relationships, or job positions. When was the last time you had a spiritual moment?

You don't need to go to the top of a mountain. It is enough to reserve a moment to connect with yourself and your beliefs, history, and goals. Some people find this moment in prayer, others by attending worship, church, mosque, or synagogue, some in the company of a meditation group and others while arranging their garden. That's how diverse we are!

The important thing is to recognize the "why" of our life, the reason for our effort, and the purpose of our existence. Sometimes, we submit to the decision of a supreme being who cares for us and accompanies us in our tribulations. I call it prayer! But you can call it whatever you want. You save a moment in the day, or at least in the week, to meditate and connect with what is most important to you. Amen! (So be it.)

Personally, I'll share with you that in my house, I have a small altar that looks more like a family tree, with photographs of my grandparents and my parents. Most of them have already passed away, and I remember them smiling as they appear in their pictures. During the day, I reserve a moment to talk with them. Sometimes I tell them about my day and worries, and I wonder what they would do in my place. That often makes me smile! I am proud to carry their legacy, and I imagine they smile from heaven when they see me. I'm never alone!

In the morning, I ask God to enlighten me and help me find the talent required to face what troubles me, and I offer a short prayer to start my day. Sometimes that prayer happens while I walk my dog in the park, while I tend to my plants, when I'm stuck in traffic, or when I sit in bed looking out the window. In any case, the important thing is to connect with yourself. Have you never done it? Try it!

Another way to connect with spirituality is gratitude. I love to keep a diary of things I am grateful for. In a world where we are bombarded with bad news and fed collective anxiety with bad omens on TV and social media, it is important to have a counterattack. For me, that is gratitude.

An exercise that I feel enriches my life a lot is the bottle exercise; I am not talking about drinking, I am referring to a positive psychology exercise which consists of having a transparent bottle in which I place small pieces of paper with the good things that happen to me during the year. From achieving objectives to a good party, a visit from a good friend, and even some minor accident that later becomes a funny memory.

My son recently obtained his driver's license, and a few months into driving, he had an accident on his way to work due to distraction. Fortunately, no injuries occurred, and the mechanic shop repaired the vehicle damage. Funny enough, the incident was captured on a dashcam, revealing that he was listening to a Mexican song then. A few days after the accident, my wife and I playfully sing that song to make him uncomfortable. I acknowledge that some might view this as a less-than-ideal action on my part, but it reflects the sense of humour we share and practice within our home. It was once a bad situation but is now part of the family history, and we remember it with a smile. After all, it could've been much worse.

Stories like these fill the bottle throughout the year, and on a special date, in my case at Christmas, we open it and begin to remember each and every one of the moments lived during those twelve months.

The gratitude bottle achieves several goals. On the one hand, it allows me to pause and say thank you for a good time. In addition, it is a visual reference that allows me to remember that there were good times during the year. Even on a bad day, I can turn to my bottle and remember that not everything has been so bad. Finally, the bottle allows us to celebrate a cycle of good things. Make your thank-you bottle!

[PICTURE OF MY BOTTLES]

In a Nicaraguan company, we adapted this exercise to the organizational setting by placing a thank-you bottle in a department. During the year, we are placing specific thanks to the team members. It has become an excellent way to satisfy recognition in work teams.

Gratitude is an excellent wellness tool. How much energy

we waste on fear, uncertainty, and anger is amazing. It is important to exercise the muscle of gratitude. If you want a gratitude journal, you can look for 30 Days of Gratitude by Jaime Leal on Amazon, and I'm sure you'll like it.

So, when was the last time you connected with your spirituality or religious practice? How often do you stop to meditate about your purpose in life? How do you rate yourself in your spiritual category?

6

Putting it all together

Assess your fire

Now that we have reviewed the categories of well-being (SPW), it is time to carry out an introspection exercise and self-assess the state of each category in our lives. You may want to return to the previous exercises to collect the necessary information and answer the questions.

Grab a glass of your favourite drink, take a deep breath and give yourself the gift of evaluating each of the six categories of the subjective perception of well-being. Good luck!

Please note that some categories may or may not apply to both environments. Up to you to decide. (i.e. your health may be the same in both spaces, while evaluating your career on a personal bonfire may be a little challenging)

Personal Bonfire

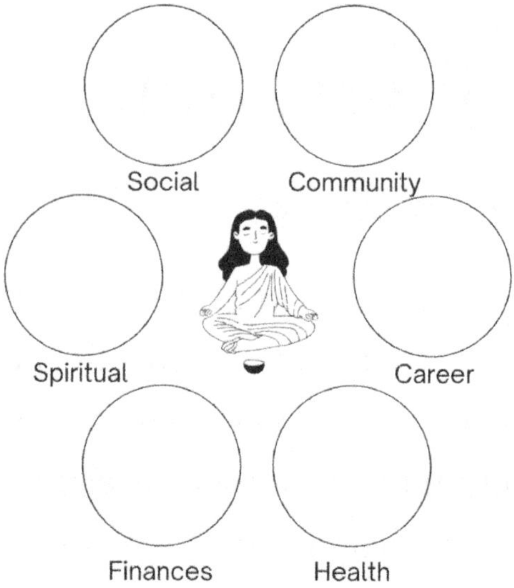

Professional bonfire

What comes to your mind as you see the evaluation? You can use the following space to write your thoughts:

We will leave your results for now. Don´t worry; we will come back to review them later. In the meantime, I invite you to learn about the triangles of wellness.

7

The triangles of wellbeing

WHAT YOU CAN AND CAN'T CONTROL

As mentioned throughout this book, happiness depends on you, but well-being does not, at least not completely.

For the necessary elements of well-being to be present in our lives, we have to approach the problem in three different dimensions, which I call *triangles of well-being*:

- Triangle of social welfare
- Triangle of well-being at Work
- Triangle of personal wellbeing

Different things influence each of these triangles and contain elements that determine how easy it is to access the integral well-being of an individual and ignite the flame of happiness.

In the macro, we can see the social welfare triangle, which considers elements of the community, the government and society in general; a smaller triangle is the triangle of well-being at work, which includes the relationship between the company, its leaders and their collaborators; finally, we have the personal wellbeing triangle, in which we must balance our personal and family priorities.

These three triangles constantly interact, determining how easy it is to access wellness. Let's explore each of them!

Social welfare triangle

It is important not to confuse the triangle of social well-being with the category of the subjective perception of social well-being. They are two different things.

Social triangle side A – The government

Since our circumstances dictate our definition of well-being and happiness, we cannot judge someone from a different context. Let me tell you a story!

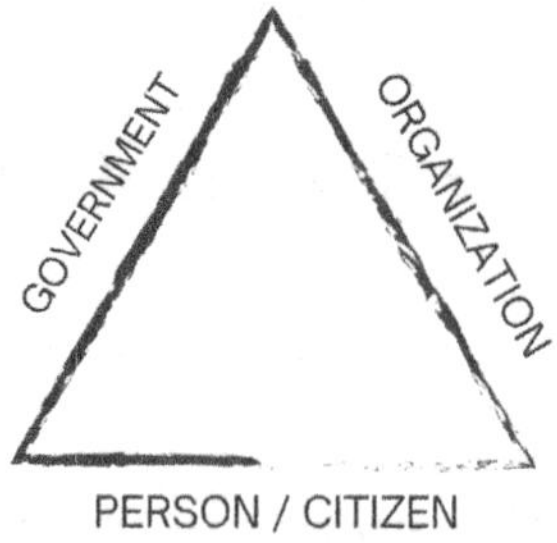

Social welfare triangle

After one of my humanitarian rescue missions, some friends got together to throw a welcome party. One of the most luxurious restaurants in northern Mexico would be the meeting point. As it's natural, my friends arrived ordering various drinks and appetizers.

During that mission, I had spent more than 45 days sleeping in a small tent, listening to how the rodents sought to enter following the aroma of the remains of food (it is the only time I have seen so many mice colliding against others trying to run away when I pointed the flashlight at them). We didn't have enough water to drink, much less to bathe; I had barely showered twice in all that time.

Resources were also scarce. I remember having hidden a small bottle of water, barely 500 ml, as I planned to share it with two children in case the drinking water was not replenished at the hospital where I worked; the situation was that difficult!

In the hospital warehouse, a small tent with cardboard boxes everywhere was Baptiste's office, a young man from Haiti, approximately 20 years old, who barely earned a dollar a day's work whilst maintaining our warehouse's medicine and supplies inventory.

Sometimes I would stop in front of the small wooden desk where Baptiste worked. We would talk about his life in Haiti before the earthquake and various topics, and on one occasion, he even asked me to give him access to the condoms that had arrived as a donation; he was having a rendezvous. We trusted each other!

One of the afternoons that I walked by his desk, he called me by blinking and pointing his lips towards inside the tent. When I got closer, I realized that he was pointing toward a bucket that he had very close to his chair.

"What is it?" I asked.

"Ice!" he replied while smiling.

"Where did you get it? Well, better not tell me; I'll quickly go for a small glass so you can give me a piece." I quickly went to my tent, where I kept the small glass that I tried to keep as clean as possible and ran back to where he was, and he served me a piece of ice with a little water.

What a moment! The two of us sat beside each other, looking at the small tents that served as rooms for the patients while we enjoyed a small glass of cold water. A complete luxury!

The memory of Baptiste came to my mind when a waiter from the restaurant brought a bucket full of ice. Not only that, but there was also beer, water, and soft drinks. All at my disposal!

One of my friends took a glass, placed some ice cubes, filled it completely with water, barely took a sip and without even paying attention, threw the rest into a garden of the restaurant where we were.

At first, I felt sadness. But then, a tingling sensation sailing in my stomach began to rise towards my chest; I felt short of breath. I quickly understood that what I felt was not grief but anger.

I thought about claiming my Mexican friend for his inconsiderate act. I turned my gaze to the ice cubes lying on the grass, and I momentarily thought about picking them up, making my friend apologize. I felt ashamed thinking about Danielle, Nadege, Ramón, César, Carlos, Baptiste, and all the other human beings in that tragedy. In my mind, I apologized for being close to that irresponsible act, but on the other hand, I felt ashamed to be angry at my friend.

Fortunately, I managed to control myself in time; I used my emotional intelligence skills to filter out the negative emotions that came over me. *"My friend doesn't know; he can't understand. Ice and water have always been present in his life; he lives where those aspects of wellbeing (clean water) are always available,"* I thought.

Each country and even each geographical area faces a different triangle of social welfare; the same elements are considered, but not all of them are present, which is why I say in my lectures that the famous quote: "we are all in the same boat" should be changed to "we are all in the same storm." Some of us are on a cruise ship with all the comforts, others on a private yacht, some on a small boat and others barely have a small life jacket as they fight to stay afloat. We are not in the same boat but going through the same storm.

Governments consider that social well-being is a condition achieved, expressed in various aspects of the life of the human being. It is expressed through the following levels:

• Health,

• Education,

• Housing,

• Consumer goods,

• Urban development,

• Security,

• Environment.

With a list like this, it is easy to understand why my Mexican friend did not consider ice and clean water a fundamental good. His welfare conditions in Mexico were completely different from those in Haiti.

To a large extent, these aspects do NOT depend on the average human being; external or group mechanisms are required for them to be developed, implemented and improved. Politicians can promote security, but it depends on the state and the community working together to improve security. It depends on everyone, but not just one! (This sounds like a political campaign slogan).

To evaluate your social welfare triangle, it is important to look at how these elements are found in your city.

How do you consider each of these elements to be in your current city?

• **Your city's health rate:** _____% (Ease of access to basic services to promote, maintain and care for the health of citizens.)

To give you an idea, Health Consumer Powerhouse periodically publishes a study on European health systems: the so-called Health Consumer Index 2018 (Professor Arne Björnberg, 2018). Here 35 countries are classified according to the quality of their health systems based on 46 indicators. Here are the top-rated countries:

1. Switzerland
2. Netherlands
3. Norway
4. Denmark
5. Belgium
6. Finland

7. Luxembourg

8. Sweden

9. Austria

10. Iceland

• **Your city's education rate:** _____% (Ease of access to basic, secondary, and higher education.)

In this matter, the PISA test (the program for the international evaluation of students created by the OECD) is the most popular way of measuring education worldwide. This test assesses the reading, mathematical, and scientific competence of 15-year-old students. (OECD, Organization for Economic Cooperation and Development, Paris, 2019).

If you want to live in the countries with the best education systems, you must move to China, Singapore, Estonia, Finland or Japan. But before you start packing your bags, I invite you to keep reading; you will soon realize there is no perfect place. **Basically, immigration is about choosing the problems you want to have. Different countries, different challenges.**

• **Your city's accessibility to housing:** _____% (Ease of access to decent housing at an affordable cost.)

There is a lot to say about this topic. Demographia International Housing Affordability rates middle-income housing affordability in 92 major housing markets in eight countries: Australia, Canada, China, Ireland, New Zealand, Singapore, the United Kingdom, and the United States. (Urban Reform Institute and the Frontier Center for Public Policy, 2022).

The study explains that, without considering income, home affordability cannot be assessed with any real meaning to potential buyers. Housing affordability is the price of housing in relation to income. How affordable is housing? Let's find out!

The pandemic demand shock: There has been an unprecedented deterioration in housing affordability during the pandemic. Severely unaffordable markets increased by 60% in 2021 compared to 2019, the last year before the COVID-19 pandemic.

Nationwide, the number of severely unaffordable markets increased by 2 in Canada, 3 in the United Kingdom, and 14 in the United States. Housing is a pending issue in the global economy! If you are short on a housing budget, you do not want to go to the "Commonwealth" of the United Kingdom: neither Australia, Canada, New Zealand, or England. It seems that there is a trend; did you notice? It is practically impossible for a person with an average income to buy a house in these countries. Younger generations still live with their parents, not because they want to but because they can´t afford to buy their place.

How easy is it to access housing in the city where you live?

• **Rate the availability of consumer goods:** _____% (Ease of access to the main consumer goods: food, drinks, cleaning items and bare necessities.)

It may seem impossible, but in some countries, these goods are not available. Some countries like Venezuela, Argentina or Cuba may have citizens who have the money to purchase goods, but these are not available due to the poor economic practices of the state.

How accessible are consumer goods? Can you live on minimum wage? Do you have access to basic products and services?

• **Your city's urban development rate:** _____% (Quality of lighting, urbanization, paving and primary services such as water, electricity, gas, telephone, and internet.)

Designing a city is no easy task, but according to an article published by Arch20 (Arch20, 2022), five products of 20th-century urban planning have reached a level of grandeur that sets them apart. They are Brasilia (Brazil), Singapore City (Singapore), Chandigarh (India), Seoul (South Korea), and Copenhagen (Denmark). I love Barcelona, but since I'm not an architect or city designer, I better not state an opinion.

What these cities have in common is their well-structured design. Brasilia, for example, follows an airplane-shaped plan in which each city function (residential, civic, administrative, recreational) sits on a separate axis. The city of Singapore adopts a similar rule, with residential areas located at four cardinal points. On the other hand, the structure of Chandigarh imitates the shape of a human being, with the financial center at the head, the commercial center at its core, and the academic and recreational centers at the arms. Seoul follows feng-shui principles, and Copenhagen's design revolves around a five-finger plane, its center being the palm and five digits coming out of it (Arch20, 2022).

The urban design of the city results in reduced traffic congestion, better public transportation, and better routes for walking and cycling. How is the urbanization of your city? The evaluation you give to this segment will partially depend on that.

• **Your city's security rate:** ___________% (perception of legality and respect for current laws, personal safety, and property security.)

The third iteration of the Safe Cities Index report classifies 60 cities according to 57 indicators that range from digital security, health safety, infrastructure security, and personal safety.

Tokyo holds first place in general, and cities from the Asia-Pacific area occupy six spots in its top 10. Still, geographical regions don't show a statistical correlation with the results. Other cities in the top 10 are Singapore (2nd place), Osaka (3rd place), Sidney (5th place), Seoul (8th place), and Melbourne (10th place). Amsterdam (4th place) and Copenhagen (tying with Seoul in the 8th place) are two European cities in this group. In comparison, two American cities complete the list, Toronto (6th place) and Washington DC (7th place) (Safe Cities Index 2019, 2019). Canada might have expensive homes, but the environment is safe; you can´t have it all!

How safe do you feel in your city? Do you live "on pins and needles"? Do you feel confident and secure that you can achieve what you dream of?

• **Your city's environmental quality rate:** _______% (Perception of care and respect for the environment. Respect towards recycling resources and ecology programmes.)

On June 14th, 2022, Arcadis released the 5th edition of its long-standing report, Arcadis Sustainable Cities Index 2022 (ARCADIS, 2022). The report shows that cities need to work toward sustainability to be truly prosperous in a world that faces a series of challenges such as climate change, over-urbanization and a decrease in resources. Arcadis Sustainable Cities Index 2022 examines 100 cities worldwide and takes on a holistic angle to highlight the ever-changing challenges these cities face.

The top 10 cities in the Arcadis Sustainable Cities Index 2022 are:

- Oslo
- Stockholm
- Tokyo
- Copenhagen
- Berlin
- London
- Seattle
- Paris
- San Francisco
- Amsterdam

This index measures three pillars. **The planet pillar** assesses the quality of a city's natural environment; European cities monopolize this planet pillar: except for Tokyo, Montreal, Los

Angeles and Bogota, the entire top 20 is made up of cities in Europe. **The people pillar** measures the quality of the social infrastructure in a city. Europe is also the clear leader in this pillar, with Western European cities occupying 15 of the top 20 places. Seoul, Singapore and Tokyo all rank in the top 10. **The profit pillar** measures the quality of the economy in a city. US cities are by far the best performers in this pillar, although most of these cities have relatively low scores in the planet and people pillars. If you want to see the full report, you can go to the Arcadis page. (ARCADIS, 2022).

Have you already decided where you will have to move to? Just kidding! There is no perfect city, and, to a large extent, these well-being elements are also highly dynamic. For instance, countries that previously had excellent security can suffer sudden riots or sudden catastrophic events that turn them highly insecure.

Knowing the state of social welfare in your city will give you a better perception of why you do or do not have access to welfare. However, remember, you can be happy anywhere; it might be more difficult in some places, but not impossible.

There is no single place where all the elements the government and the community must offer for social welfare coincide. We can also note that these elements do not depend directly on a citizen but rather on the work of all citizens together.

It is now time to move to the second side of the triangle of social welfare, businesses, and organizations!

Social triangle side B – the business side

In more recent times, organizations have been working to increase the general well-being of their employees. At the Canadian Emotional Paycheck Institute, we have a psychological measurement that allows us to understand the current state of a company's well-being and accurately measure whether they have the necessary elements to generate well-being and a good emotional salary. The elements of emotional salary are:

- **Tools and equipment:** possessing the necessary equipment to carry out the tasks assigned to the employees.
- **Expectations for the future:** Expected growth and an action plan with realistic goals to develop professionally in the company.

- **Financial salary:** receiving competitive financial compensation for the employee's work and responsibilities within the company.

- **Employee life cycle:** being recognized by the company during the different stages that the employee lives, from hiring to termination.

- **Work-life balance:** the balance that the employee can enjoy between personal and work life, allowing spaces for rest and recreation.

- **Organizational culture:** living in a pleasant environment with positive relationships allows employees to live their values and exercise their skills while contributing to the organization's success.

- **Personal growth:** enjoying growth on a personal level that allows the employee to develop other skills and competencies that will allow them to be a better person.

- **Learning challenge:** finding sufficiently motivating and realistic challenges that keep employees interested in their work.

- **Relationship with the immediate boss:** this is so important that we have dedicated its side of the triangle to it... We will see it later.

Each of these elements must be present in the organization

to promote the well-being of the workers at a professional level.

As we can see, in this triangle of social well-being, we have little interference; the society in general and large corporations must act to generate the necessary elements to enjoy well-being. However, not all is lost. There is another small triangle that we will analyze next, the triangle of well-being at work.

Triangle of well-being at work

In this triangle, much smaller than the triangle of social well-being, we can find the elements the company contributes to employee well-being. We will also find the skills of the immediate supervisor to promote them. Finally, the employees themselves execute their well-being within the world of work.

Triangle of well-being at work

Work triangle side A – The company

On this side of the triangle, we have to place eight of the nine well-being elements described in the previous triangle, as they are a company's contribution to the well-being of its people. The last element, the relationship with the immediate boss, is so important for the well-being of people that it ends up occupying an entire side of the work triangle.

If you want to know the level of well-being offered by the organization in which you work, use the Tarrix test, the first in the world to measure the emotional salary in an organization. (Scan the QR code and access a complimentary sample)

Social triangle side B – The immediate supervisor

As I have mentioned in this chapter already, an employee's relationship with their immediate boss plays a fundamental role in their well-being, from the high levels of stress that a bad relationship with them can bring, to the imbalance between personal and professional life, to name a few.

How to know if you have a good boss? Here are some questions for you to evaluate.

• Are they willing to try new things?

• Do they treat you and your colleagues as human beings with other priorities besides work?

• Do they show favouritism within the work environment?

• Are they good mediators in cases of conflict? Can you talk to your boss about the problems you are facing at work?

• Do you hold at least one meeting every six months in which you talk about your personal and professional growth? Do you trust that your boss works for your professional growth?

• Do they accept recommendations regarding the problems you all face in the organization?

• Do they have a good sense of humour?

• Do they genuinely care about your goals?

• Do they offer you the digital disconnection you need during your days off?

You may have a great boss if you say yes to all these questions.

This is one of the determining elements for your well-being, as the immediate boss becomes the spokesperson for the benefits of working for an organization. I love training middle managers in companies because they are where the changes take place, where the culture is forged, and where the organization's environment is fully lived.

How is your relationship with your immediate boss? Do you think you have a good boss who facilitates your well-being?

Well, it's time to address the last of the triangles, the triangle of personal wellness.

*Your original copy of this book allows you access to the psychological test that measures the well-being that a company can offer you. Just go to www.emotionalpaycheck.com/tarrix and enter the WGSOP code, and you will get your results automatically in your email.

Personal wellness triangle

This is the smallest of the wellness triangles, but it is special because it allows us to balance the personal elements that allow us access to well-being and happiness.

On one side, you will find a job; on the other, the family; and on the last, the person. How do you find yourself in each of these elements? How do you manage to balance these priorities? Are there times when you take too much care of one of these sides of the triangle, neglecting the other two? Let's check!

Triangle of personal well-being side A - Work

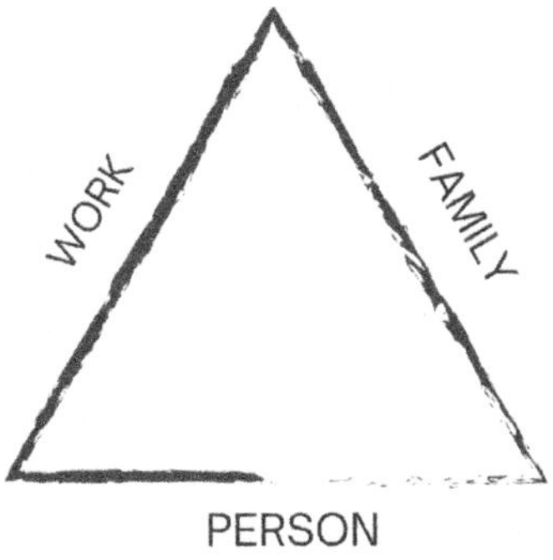

Personal wellness triangle

On this side, we find all the professional responsibilities an individual must fulfill to have the necessary economic income for their family and personal needs. You can evaluate this side based on the qualification you gave to the same side of the other two triangles (Government and Business).

Triangle of personal well-being side B - The family

On this side of the triangle, we will find the personal responsibilities that the individual has with friends and family, as well as the time they invest in social activities.

How much time do you spend with the people you love? How much do you enjoy the balance between work life and personal life? How long has it been since you had free time to spend with those closest to you? Now is a good moment to analyze it.

Triangle of personal well-being – side C - The person

Surely you have noticed that in the previous triangles, we omitted the C side of the triangle. This is because it is the same person who interacts in the three triangles, and it is now that we will analyze what their needs are and how they are found.

To measure wellness on this side of the triangle, you will use the ratings given to your self-perceived well-being in the six categories we mentioned in the previous chapter.

• Social Category: how do you evaluate the amount of love you receive from the people closest to you?

• Community Category: how do you evaluate the quality of your interpersonal relationships with friends and family?

• Career Category: How do you rate the use of your professional skills in the job you currently do?

• Financial category: how do you assess the quality of your finances?

• Health category: how do you rate your physical and emotional health?

• Spiritual category: how do you evaluate your contact with your spirituality?

Based on this evaluation, you will be able to determine your rating for this very important side of the triangle, which, of course, is at the base of all triangles as the main reason we measure well-being in the first place: the person.

Well-being can be likened to having access to the six elements needed to "start a fire," while happiness is the conscious decision to ignite it. **Yes, happiness is ultimately a choice we make.**

Dr. Leal

8

Lighting the bonfire

Unleash, radiate, ignite

In this section, you will have access to a series of questions that will allow you to plan the necessary following actions to light your wellness bonfire.

We now realize that we have made a journey through what depends and what does not depend directly on you. (Triangles of well-being) This is a fundamental step to gain access to the well-being of the individual, as many times we lose ourselves worrying about what we do not have control over, and we waste valuable time that we could use to improve what we can, in fact, control.

With your knowledge, you can make sure that you have these six elements of well-being present in your life and even determine if it is necessary to work on improving any of the elements found in larger triangles (work or social). For example, if after analyzing your chances to light your bonfire of wellness, you discover that you don't have the necessary elements in the well-being triangle at work, it may be time to have a conversation with your boss or, in the worst-case scenario, start looking for a new job. On the other hand, some people may discover that they are in a community where the elements of the triangle of social welfare are unavailable, leading them to think about migrating to other environments for a greater benefit.

In 2010, I was kidnapped, I have reasons to believe that my captors had some kind of military or police background, and I lost all confidence in what the government could do to provide me with the security I required and, more importantly, for my family. Without realizing it, it was at that time that I understood that the social welfare triangle, specifically the government side, could not be improved for me. So, I decided to emigrate to another country that offered better conditions for my wellness in the social triangle.

Some of my friends and relatives still live and thrive in the same city. Once again, the measurement of these triangles is completely individual and subjective. Even if they live in the same city, everyone has their own triangles!

Great decisions can be made with much greater clarity when we are aware of the elements we lack and can determine if those elements we need to light the fire of well-being depend on us.

Will it be necessary to emigrate to another country? Will we have to change jobs? Will we work on the promotion of a certain law? Will we acquire tools to increase the possibilities of well-being? Is it just a matter of making a conscious decision to be happy? Do we have what it takes to do so? Are we ready to light the bonfire of wellness? These are some of the questions that I am sure you can now answer much more clearly.

The Wellness bonfire is available if you have the elements to light it. Although it is sometimes difficult to accept it, there are situations in which these elements are not available, and we will have to move to look for them or even build them ourselves.

To get the most out of this book, I suggest the following exercise:

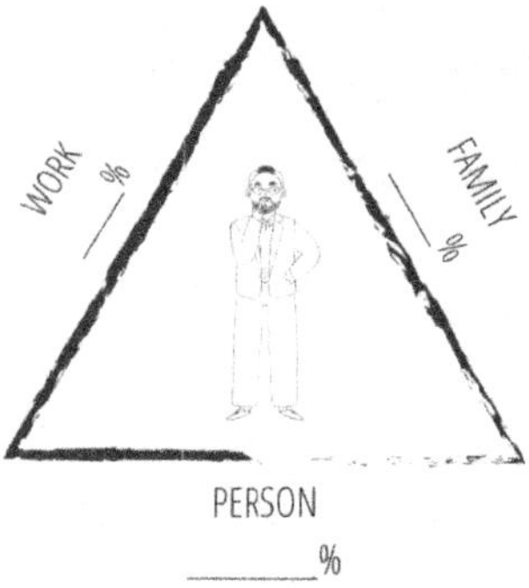

PERSONAL WELLNESS TRIANGLE

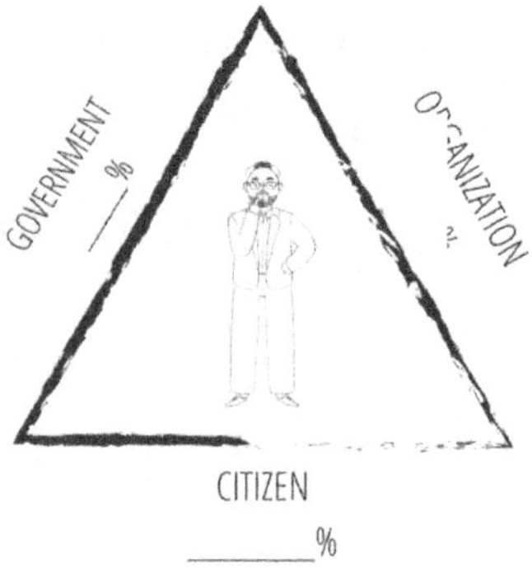

SOCIAL WELFARE TRIANGLE

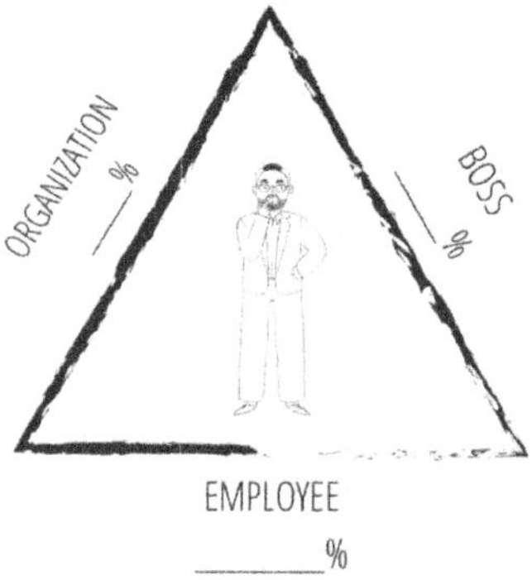

TRIANGLE OF WELL-BEING AT WORK

On a scale from 1% to 100%, where 1% is terrible and 100% is excellent, how would you evaluate each of these sides of the triangles of wellness?

1. Rate each of the triangles in the suggested order (social, work and personal):

Once you have evaluated each triangle:

a. Identify the triangle with the greatest areas of opportunity;

b. Define how much control you have over the areas of opportunity;

c. Identify the advantages that each triangle presents;

d. Define how you can benefit from the strengths of each triangle;

2. Rate each of the categories of the subjective perception of wellbeing

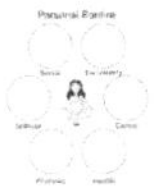

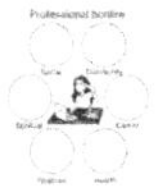

Go back to Page 87

Go back to retrieve the grades you gave on each of these categories. (Image for reference)

Answer the next support questions:

What category has the highest evaluation? Why do you think it does?

What category has the lowest evaluation? Why do you think it does?

Now, select the category (or categories) with the lowest evaluation and think of at least two strategies to improve that category. (Write them next)

3. Review your progress within a period of no more than six months.

Just like Rome was not built in one day, happiness is an

ongoing process that requires attention, perseverance and continuous improvement. Make sure you come back to this evaluation frequently.

9

Leadership of well-being

To become a true well-being bonfire leader, it is necessary for you to first work on your bonfire. However, it will also be important for you to start working on facilitating the well-being bonfire of your team.

Here are some ideas that may be of interest to help you become a leader who promotes well-being in your organization. Some of these ideas can be easily applied, even without financial investment, while others require management authorization. Here we go!

There is no more powerful tool for increasing emotional engagement than conversing with your teammates. Make sure you listen twice as much as you speak.

How to increase the social category within your team

One-on-one meetings: Organize one-on-one meetings with your team members. Make sure they speak more than you do during the meeting. You can use the 3-question system for the one-on-one meetings:

1. What have I been doing well as a leader that you would like me to continue doing?

2. What have I not done enough that you would like me to do a bit more?

3. How can I make your work easier and more efficient?

By asking these three questions, you will gain access to much more information about how you can help your team members feel valued.

Practice positive feedback: Don't become a leader who only talks to their team when things go wrong. Make sure to schedule rounds to recognize progress and achievements regularly. That way, when the time comes to provide negative feedback, your team will be more receptive.

Have you heard about feed-forward? Feed-forward is a concept that focuses on providing guidance and suggestions for future improvement rather than dwelling on past mistakes or shortcomings. It involves offering constructive feedback and recommendations to help individuals or teams enhance their performance and achieve better results in the future. Interesting, right? You may want to give it a try!

Unlike traditional feedback, which typically involves discussing past actions and behaviours, feed-forward shifts the focus to future actions and desired outcomes. It encourages proactive thinking and empowers individuals to make positive changes and grow professionally.

How to increase the community category within your team

Integration activities: Integration activities don't have to take place outside the company premises or last the entire day. You can incorporate small exercises that allow us to get to know each other better beyond the work environment. Reserve a small portion of some work meetings to chat about trivial topics or even engage in activities that allow for sharing more about our personal lives.

Virtual coffee: Promote an activity among your team members where they can have virtual coffee meetings. We know that many companies nowadays operate in remote environments, which makes it difficult to build a sense of community within a company. I'm sure many team members would welcome such an initiative. Remember that one of the main motivations of human beings is the sense of belonging.

How to increase the career category within your team

Life and career plan: Have one-on-one meetings where the main topic of discussion is the employee's professional future within the organization. When employees don't perceive themselves as part of the organization's plans, demotivation sets in, and the likelihood of increased staff turnover exponentially rises. Hold one-on-one meetings to explain the life and career plan compared to the organization's indicators and the competencies the employee needs to develop.

E.F.C. - There is a tool called Emotional Paycheck developed by the Canadian Institute specifically designed to find the balance between challenge and learning, which is essential for achieving a state of flow. You can find more information about this tool on our YouTube channel.

Active breaks are crucial for individuals who spend long hours working in front of a computer

How to increase the physical and emotional category within your team

Digital disconnection: As we have learned in this book, the American Psychological Association found 9 out of 10 doctor visits are related to stress. This high-stress level is largely due to interconnectivity with social media and electronic devices that keep us tied to work, even during our days off. How about implementing a digital disconnection program? Promote not sending work-related emails during rest hours and remind everyone to disconnect. Well-being is everyone's responsibility.

Active breaks: Despite being frequently mentioned, it is necessary to make active breaks, which include breathing exercises and stretches, part of the work culture. This will help reduce cortisol levels and increase employees' physical and emotional well-being. Give it a try!

Gratitude exercises: One of the key tools in positive psychology is practicing gratitude exercises. These exercises may seem simple but have great depth. Gratitude exercises help generate the hormones necessary for happiness. You can implement some exercises through a gratitude journal or by allocating a few minutes in meetings to share what everyone is grateful for. Make it part of your culture!

Analysis of workload: Unfortunately, many organizations assign more work to those employees who deliver the best results. This often leads to an overload that can result in burnout for top performers. Review the workload distribution and ensure it is equitable within the organizational structure.

Education: Most physical and mental health challenges at work are linked to education. Many subjects are still unknown to employees, so organizations need to play a proactive role in promoting these topics.

Financial education is one of the neglected subjects within the formal education system.

How to increase the financial category within your team

Financial education: Financial literacy is one of the areas lacking in formal education. People have access to information about artificial intelligence and robotics, but for some reason, they don't understand how their credit cards work. Educate your staff in finance to help them make better use of their budgets. They will appreciate it! Some topics that might be interesting for employees include:

- Learning to manage a credit card.
- Learning to manage and administer a mortgage.
- Learning to calculate interest rates when making a purchase.
- Learning to create a family budget.

Encouraging savings through implementing solar panels, energy-efficient light bulbs, and electric vehicles, among other things. Remember that financial education is not just about income but also about managing it. There is never enough money for someone who doesn't know how to manage it.

Regarding the spiritual category

Spirituality is personal, so we suggest not addressing it directly in the workplace. However, a diversity and inclusion campaign that recognizes different religious beliefs and gives them appropriate value and significance is crucial for overall well-being. Make sure to be inclusive in your communications and religious celebrations.

With these ideas, you will have a better chance to increase well-being and facilitate the bonfire of your team members. If you want to accurately assess the areas of well-being that need reinforcement in your company, I have a gift for you at the end of this book. The first assessment measures your emotional paycheck, and a free sample awaits you at the end of this book.

Conclusion

A Brief Summary

People can be happy in any environment. However, certain elements allow us to have easier access to happiness. These elements are the categories of the subjective perception of well-being (SPW).

In this book, we have addressed each of these categories, coming up with ideas on how to improve them at a personal and work level. Now that you know the necessary elements to light your bonfire of well-being, it is your responsibility to start, control and fan that fire of wellness in your life.

Wellness is a work in progress: as with any campfire, we must keep an eye on it, throw in a little more wood when it is about to become extinguished, and sometimes even light it back. We know that sometimes winds and storms threaten to put it out and that some of the items we need to build will be in short supply. However, if we pay attention, we will always find a way to keep it burning but remember: once the bonfire of wellbeing is lit, the flames must be fanned well, "wood" has to be fed now and then; otherwise, your bonfire will turn to ashes.

I'm not good with goodbyes, so I'll assume that you'll write me a message, that we'll see each other walking our dogs, or that you'll invite me to speak at an event. By the way, I have a gift for you; find it on the next page.

See you later!

Introducing Tarrix: The groundbreaking assessment that unveils the true essence of workplace satisfaction - the Emotional Paycheck. With Tarrix, you can now measure the nine crucial elements that form the foundation of a high emotional paycheck within any company or organization. But that's not all. Tarrix also assesses the six key elements of well-being that every employee needs to unlock the path to happiness and understand their own motivations.

Experience the power of this simple yet remarkable artificial intelligence tool that brings clarity and insight to your work life. Take advantage of our limited-time offer and get a free sample of Tarrix at app.tarrix.ai or scan the QR code below. Don't miss out on this opportunity to revolutionize your workplace and discover the secrets to a fulfilling career. Use the code provided to unlock the full potential of Tarrix. Take control of your emotional paycheck today!

Use the code: 5A3A3

About the Author

Jaime Leal

Dr. Leal is a dedicated professional based in the picturesque town of Niagara Falls, Ontario. As Director of The Emotional Paycheck®, an esteemed online institute, Dr. Leal passionately connects the realms of happiness and return on investment.

With a diverse educational background, Dr. Leal holds a Bachelor's degree in Marketing and Advertising, a Bachelor's degree in Psychology, and two Master's degrees in Negotiation and Positive Education. These academic achievements reflect Dr. Leal's commitment to understanding the intricacies of human emotions and well-being.

As an author, Dr. Leal has contributed significantly to the field with his work, including the influential Emotional Paycheck Method and the inspiring book "30 Days of Gratitude," both available on Amazon.

Beyond his professional endeavours, Dr. Leal is driven by a deep sense of compassion. He has selflessly volunteered as a Humanitarian Relief Volunteer, assisting during Haiti's devastating earthquake in 2010. Dr. Leal received the prestigious Exemplary Citizen Award for his exceptional service from Pazes N.G.O. and the LOGRO Award from the University of Tec Milenio.

Dr. Leal's expertise and insights have also been shared on the renowned TEDx stage, where they have captivated audiences with his thought-provoking talks.

Would you like to unlock the secrets to workplace well-being and enhance productivity and happiness among your team? Dr. Jaime Leal invites you to explore the transformative power of his masterclasses and workshops.

Discover how to create a thriving work environment, implement effective well-being strategies, and ignite the bonfire of well-being in your organization. Dr. Leal's expertise and methodology are proven to enhance employee satisfaction and performance.

www.emotionalpaycheck.com

jaime@emotionalpaycheck.com

References

Aban Tamayo, J., Becerra Pérez, M., Delajara, M., León Robles, I. (2020). El estándar de ingreso mínimo en cuatro grandes ciudades de México [The minimum income standard in four major cities in Mexico]. Centro de Estudios Espinosa Yglesias. https://ceey.org.mx/el-estandar-de-ingreso-minimo-en-cuatro-grandes-ciudades-de-mexico/

Allen, R. (2013). Poverty Lines in History, Theory, and Current International Practice. No 685, Economics Series Working Papers, University of Oxford, Department of Economics. https://EconPapers.repec.org/RePEc:oxf:wpaper:685.

Allen, R. C. (2017). Absolute poverty: When necessity displaces desire. American Economic Review, 107(12), 3690-3721. https://doi.org/10.1257/aer.20161080

Aquino, T. D. (n.d.). Suma de Teología, I, II, (Vol. q. 2, a. 1-7.)

Arch20. (2022, December 2023). ARCH20 - 5 well planned cities. Retrieved from Arch20: https://www.arch2o.com/well-planned-cities-20th-century/

Aristóteles. (2001). Ética a Nicómaco [Nicomachean Ethics].

(J. Calvo, Trans.) (1st Ed.). Alianza Editorial. (Original work published 349 BCE)

Aristóteles / Moral a Nicómaco / versión de Patricio de Azcárate, Madrid. (1873). Filosofia. Retrieved April 5, 2021, from: https://www.filosofia.org/cla/ari/azc01.htm

Asch, S. E. (1951). Effects of group pressure upon the modification and distortion of judgments. In H. Guetzkow (Ed.), Groups, leadership, and men (pp.177-190). Pittsburgh, PA: Carnegie.

Augustine, S. (1470). The City of God. (M. Duds, Trans.) Digi reads.com.

Aulinas A. (2019). Physiology of the Pineal Gland and Melatonin. [Updated 2019 Dec 10]. In: Feingold KR, Anawalt B, Boyce A, et al., editors. Endotext [Internet]. South Dartmouth (MA): MDText.com, Inc.; 2000-. Retrieved from: https://www.ncbi.nlm.nih.gov/books/NBK550972/

Ayalon, L. (2017, January 5). Taking a closer look at ageism: self- and other-directed ageist attitudes and discrimination. SpringerLink. https://tinyurl.com/mrf69s7k

Bennis, W., & Nanus, B. (1985). Leaders: The Strategies for Taking Charge. Harper & Row; 1st edition. ISBN 978-0060152468.

Benson, A., Li, D., & Shue, K. (2019). Promotions and the

Peter Principle*. The Quarterly Journal of Economics, 134(4), 2085–2134. https://doi.org/10.1093/qje/qjz02218

Björnberg, A. P. (2018). Euro health consumer index 2018.

Harvard Business Review. (2014, August 7). Blockbuster Becomes a Casualty of Big Bang Disruption. Retrieved from https://hbr.org/2013/11/blockbuster-becomes-a-casualty-of-big-bang-disruption

Buehner, C. W. (1971). Richard Evans' Quote Book. Publisher's Press.

Cirillo, F. (2007). The Pomodoro Technique. CreateSpace Independent Publishing Platform.

Coneval. (2018). Programas de calculo y bases de datos 2008, 2010, 2012, 2014, 2016 y 2018 [Calculation programs and databases 2008, 2010, 2012, 2014, 2016, and 2018]. Retrieved from https://www.coneval.org.mx/Medicion/MP/Paginas/Programas_BD_08_10_12_14_16_18.aspx

Council on Communications and Media. (2016). Media and Young Minds. Pediatrics, 138(5), e20162591. https://doi.org/10.1542/peds.2016-2591

Cronbach, L. J. (1951). Coefficient alpha and the internal structure of tests. Psychometrika, 16, 297-334.

Csikszentmihalyi, M. (1990). Flow: The psychology of optimal experience. New York: Harper-Perennial.

Covey, S. R. (2020). The 7 Habits of Highly Effective People: Powerful Lessons in Personal Change (anniversary). Simon & Schuster.

Diversity is Being Invited to the Party: Inclusion is Being Asked to Dance. (2015, December 10). [Video]. YouTube. https://www.youtube.com/watch?v=9gS2VPUkB3M

Does school prepare students for the real world? This teen speaker says no. (2015, November 8). TED-Ed Blog. Retrieved https://blog.ed.ted.com/2015/08/25/does-school-prepare-students-for-the-real-world-this-teen-speaker-says-no/

Doran, G. T. (1981). "There's a S.M.A.R.T. Way to Write Management's Goals and Objectives". Management Review, 70(11), 35-36.

Dudley, G., Banister, D., & Schwanen, T. (2017). The Rise of Uber and Regulating the Disruptive Innovator. The Political Quarterly, 88, 492-499. https://doi.org/10.1111/1467-923X.12373

Dunbar, R. I. M. (2010). How many friends does one person need?: Dunbar's number and other evolutionary quirks. London: Faber and Faber. ISBN 978-0-571-25342-5

Enciclopedia-juridica.com. (2020). Derecho consuetudinario [Customary law]. Enciclopedia jurídica. Retrieved from http s://bit.ly/3rG4srh

Glassdoor. (2017). Glassdoor Survey Finds Americans Forfeit Half Of Their Earned Vacation/Paid Time Off. Glassdoor About Us. Retrieved from https://bit.ly/3Ol9iUR

Global poverty: A first estimation of its uncertainty. (2021, June 1). ScienceDirect. https://shorturl.gg/yhLp

Growth and poverty in developing countries. (1979, January 1). ScienceDirect. Retrieved from https://www.sciencedirect.com/science/article/abs/pii/0304387879900208

Harber, V. J., & Sutton, J. R. (1984). Endorphins and exercise. Sports Med, 1(2), 154-171. doi: 10.2165/00007256-198401020-00004. PMID: 6091217.

Hardy, Q. (2016, November 25). The New Workplace Is Agile, and Nonstop. Can You Keep Up? The New York Times. Retrieved from https://www.nytimes.com/2016/11/25/technology/the-new-workplace-is-agile-and-nonstop-can-you-keep-up.html

HRD Connect. (2019). Katherine Phillips, Columbia Business School: Why Diverse Teams are Smarter. HRD Live Podcasts. Retrieved from https://tinyurl.com/yeyfwkrj

Inegi.org (2022). Encuesta Nacional de Ocupación y Empleo (ENOE), población de 15 años y más de edad [National Survey of Occupation and Employment (ENOE), population aged

15 years and older]. Retrieved from https://www.inegi.org.mx/programas/enoe/15ymas/

Jha, A. K. (2020). Understanding Generation Alpha. https://doi.org/10.31219/osf.io/d2e8g

Kant, I. (2012). Fundamentación para una metafísica de las costumbres [Grounding for the Metaphysics of Morals]. (R. Rodríguez, Trans.) (2nd ed.). Alianza Editorial. (Original work published 1785)

Kant, I. (2013). Crítica de la razón práctica [Critique of Practical Reason]. (R. Rodríguez, Trans.) (2nd ed.). Alianza Editorial. (Original work published 1788)

Kennedy, S., & Ruggles, S. (2014). Breaking up is hard to count: the rise of divorce in the United States, 1980-2010. Demography, 51(2), 587–598. https://doi.org/10.1007/s13524-013-0270-9

Kohler, S. (2021). Potentials and Limitations of Educational Videos on YouTube for Science Communication. Frontiers. Retrieved from https://www.frontiersin.org/articles/10.3389/fcomm.2021.581302/full

Lao-Tzu. (2017). Tao Te Ching. (G. García, Trans.). Alianza editorial. (Original work published in Chinese, 4th century BCE)

Lapierre, M. A., Piotrowski, J. T., & Linebarger, D. L. (2012).

Background television in the homes of US children. Pediatrics, 130(5), 839–846. https://doi.org/10.1542/peds.2011-2581

Leal G., J. (2021). The Emotional Salary Method: How to Give a Raise Without Affecting the Budget. Emotional Paycheck Publishing.

Lee, H. J., Macbeth, A. H., Pagani, J. H., & Young, W. S., 3rd (2009). Oxytocin: the great facilitator of life. Progress in Neurobiology, 88(2), 127–151. Retrieved from https://doi.org/10.1016/j.pneurobio.2009.04.001

Leonhardt, M. (2019, December 30). Millennials are making travel a priority more than previous generations—that's not a bad thing. CNBC. Retrieved from https://www.cnbc.com/2019/08/30/millennials-making-travel-a-priority-more-than-previous-generations.html

Linebarger, D. L., & Walker, D. (2005). American behavioral scientist. [Journal article]. Sage Publications.

Malone, T., Laubacher, R., & Johns, T. (2011). The Big Idea: The Age of Hyperspecialization. Harvard Business Review. Retrieved from https://hbr.org/2011/07/the-big-idea-the-age-of-hyperspecialization

Marsh, E., Perez E., & Spence A. (2022). The digital workplace and its dark side: An integrative review. Computers in Human

Behavior, 128, 107-118. ISSN 0747-5632. Retrieved from https://doi.org/10.1016/j.chb.2021.107118

Martín Pérez, F. (2002). San Juan Chamula; empire of impunity. El Universal.MX. Retrieved from https://archivo.eluniversal.com.mx/estados/46066.html

McMahon, D. M. (2006). Happiness: A history. Atlantic Monthly Press. Retrieved from https://psycnet.apa.org/record/2006-05643-000

Mill, J. S. (1984). Utilitarianism. (E. Guisán, Trans.) (1st ed.). Alianza Editorial. (Original work published 1863)

Mongrain, M., & Anselmo-Matthews, T. (2012). Do Positive Psychology Exercises Work? A Replication of Seligman et al. Journal of Clinical Psychology, 68. https://doi.org/10.1002/jclp.21839

OECD, Organisation for Economic Co-operation and Development. (2019). The PISA test. Paris, France: OECD.

Ortega y Gasset, J. (1963). Complete works of José Ortega y Gasset. Volume II. (6th Ed.). Revista de Occidente.

Passmore, H., & Holder, D. (2017). Noticing nature: Individual and social benefits of a two-week intervention. The Journal of Positive Psychology, 12(6), 537-546. https://doi.org/10.1080/17439760.2016.1221126

Peter, L. F., & Hull, R. (1969). The Peter Principle. The American Biology Teacher, 31(6), 400. https://doi.org/10.2307/4442678

Pflug, J. (2009). Folk Theories of Happiness: A Cross-Cultural Comparison of Conceptions of Happiness in Germany and South Africa. Social Indicators Research, 92, 551-563. https://doi.org/10.1007/s11205-008-9306-8.

Plato. (1981). Dialogues I: Apology. Crito. Euthyphro. Ion. Lysis. Charmides. Hippias Minor. Hippias Major. Laches. Protagoras. (J. Calonge, E. Lledó, & C. García, Trans.) (1st Ed.) (Vol. 1). Editorial Gredos. (Original work published 1578).

Pressat, R. (1967). El análisis demográfico. Fondo de Cultura Económica. Mexico City, Mexico. 440 p.

Quispe Llanos, R. J. (2021). Analysis of poverty and income distribution 2009-2016. Revista IECOS, 18, 97-142. https://doi.org/10.21754/iecos.v18i0.1178

Radesky, J. S., Schumacher, J., & Zuckerman, B. (2015). Mobile and interactive media use by young children: the good, the bad, and the unknown. Pediatrics, 135(1), 1-3. https://doi.org/10.1542/peds.2014-2251

Ramírez, E. (1994). General demography: theory, methods, and behaviors. Academia Nacional de Ciencias Económicas. Caracas (DC)-Venezuela. 311 p.

Rincón, R. D. (2012). Organizational performance indicators: a guide for their definition. Revista Universidad EAFIT, 34(111), 43-59. Retrieved from https://publicaciones.eafit.edu.co/index.php/revista-universidad-eafit/article/view/1104

Robison, J. (2008). Turning around employee turnover. Gallup Business Journal. Retrieved on June 21, 2021, from https://news.gallup.com/businessjournal/106912/turning-around-your-turnover-problem.aspx

San Francisco de Sales. (1622). Letters. Santa Juana de Chantal. Reproduced by Nabu Press (2014). Trans. Bartolomé Alcázar. ISBN 978-1293776896.

Schaefer, H. E. (2017). Music-Evoked Emotions-Current Studies. Frontiers in Neuroscience, 11, 600. Retrieved from: https://doi.org/10.3389/fnins.2017.00600

SDWorx - Salary swindle. (2017). SDWORX. Retrieved from: https://www.sdworx.com/en/blog/payroll/the-risks-of-poor-payroll-for-businesses

Seligman, M. E. P. (1972). Learned Helplessness. Annual Review of Medicine, 23(1), 407–412. https://doi.org/10.1146/annurev.me.23.020172.002203

Seligman, M. E. P. (1991). Learned Optimism: How to Change Your Mind and Your Life. New York, NY: Pocket Books.

Seligman, M. E. P., Rashid, T., & Parks, A. C. (2006). Positive psychotherapy. American Psychologist, 61, 774-788.

Seligman, M. E. P. (2011). Authentic Happiness. Barcelona: Ediciones B.

Seligman, M. E. P. (2011). Flourish. New York: Free Press. pp. 16–20. ISBN 9781439190760

Shigehiro, O. (2013). Concepts of Happiness Across Time and Cultures. Personality & Social Psychology Bulletin, 39.

Sin, N. L., & Lyubomirsky, S. (2009). Enhancing well-being and alleviating depressive symptoms with positive psychology interventions: A practice-friendly meta-analysis. Journal of Clinical Psychology, 65(5), 467-487.

Smids, J., Nyholm, S., & Berkers, H. (2019). Robots in the Workplace: a Threat to—or Opportunity for—Meaningful Work? Philosophy & Technology, 33(3), 503–522. https://doi.org/10.1007/s13347-019-00377-4

Stress in America 2020: A National Mental Health Crisis. (2020). PsycEXTRA Dataset. https://doi.org/10.1037/e509532020-001

Sutherland, W., Jarrahi, M. H., Dunn, M., & Nelson, S. B. (2020). Work Precarity and Gig Literacies in Online Freelancing. Work, Employment and Society, 34(3), 457–475. https://doi.org/10.1177/0950017019886511

Taylor, M. K. (2018). Xennials: A microgeneration in the workplace. Industrial and Commercial Training, 50(3), 136–147. https://doi.org/10.1108/ict-08-2017-0065

The Associated Press. (2019, June 7). Bookseller Barnes & Noble, humbled by Amazon, has been sold to a hedge fund. Chicagotribune.Com. Retrieved from https://www.chicagotribune.com/business/ct-biz-barnes-and-noble-sale-20190607-story.html

The rise of robots and the fall of routine jobs. (2020, October 1). ScienceDirect. Retrieved from https://www.sciencedirect.com/science/article/pii/S0927537120300890

Thoreau, H. D. (2005). Walden (J. Alcoriza & A. Lastra, Trans.; 1854 ed., Vol. 1). Cátedra.

Tomás de Aquino, S. (1988). Suma teológica (1st Ed.). Biblioteca de Autores Cristianos.

Torraco, R. J., & Lundgren, H. (2019). What HRD Is Doing—What HRD Should be Doing: The Case for Transforming HRD. Human Resource Development Review, 19(1), 39–65. https://doi.org/10.1177/1534484319877058

Tversky, A. (1972). Elimination by aspects: A theory of choice. Psychological Review, 79(4), 281–299. https://doi.org/10.1037/h0032955

Twain, M., Pinchot, B., & Blackstone Audio, Inc. (2010). Chapters from My Autobiography. Blackstone Audio, Inc.

Urban Reform Institute and the Frontier Centre for Public Policy. (2022). Demographia International Housing Affordability.

Vaupel, J. W., Villavicencio, F., & Bergeron-Boucher, M. P. (2021). Demographic perspectives on the rise of longevity. Proceedings of the National Academy of Sciences, 118(9), e2019536118. https://doi.org/10.1073/pnas.2019536118

Veyne, P. (1995). Séneca y el estoicismo (M. Utrilla, Trans.). Fondo de Cultura Económica. (Original work published 1993)

Vyas L., Butakhieo, N. (2021). The impact of working from home during COVID-19 on work and life domains: An exploratory study on Hong Kong. Policy Design and Practice, 4(1), 59-76. DOI:10.1080/25741292.2020.1863560

Wolpe, J. (1973). The Practice of Behavior Therapy (2nd ed.). Pergamon Press.

Woodard, A. (2017). The best and worst HR names. HRM The Australian news for HR. Retrieved from https://www.hrmonline.com.au/section/featured/best-worst-hr-names/

Woodworth, R. J., O'Brien-Malone, A., Diamond, M. R., & Schüz, B. (2016). Happy Days:

Philippe, F. L., Vallerand, R. J., Houlfort, N., Lavigne, G. L., &

Donahue, E. G. (2010). Passion for an activity and quality of interpersonal relationships: The mediating role of emotions. Journal of Personality and Social Psychology, 98(6), 917-932.

Positive Psychology interventions effects on affect in an N-of-1 trial. International Journal of Clinical and Health Psychology, 16(1), 21–29. Retrieved from https://doi.org/10.1016/j.ijchp.2015.07.006

World Economic Forum. (2021). The Global Risk Report 2021. World Economic Forum. Retrieved from https://www3.weforum.org/docs/WEF_The_Global_Risks_Report_2021.pdf

Made in the USA
Monee, IL
08 December 2023

48610617R00095